North American Automotive Museums:

"Touchstones" to a Precious Heritage

One of the blessings for motoring enthusiasts in this country is the number and quality of transportation museums. When *Automobile Quarterly* published the *Directory of North American Automobile Museums* in 1992, author John Heilig counted 238 auto museums in North America; 220 in the United States and 18 in Canada. Today the count eclipses 1,000. "But like the automobile manufacturers, automobile museums come and go. Some are successful and continue for years, others flash brightly for a short while and fizzle out," noted Heilig.

In each issue of *AQ/Automobile Quarterly*, we're pleased to feature in-depth stories of these "touchstones" that chronicle the epochs of transportation history. This quarter, I'm especially proud of our insightful coverage by Richard Mandel of the Packard museums that do such a magnificent job of preserving the legends and lore of one of America's great automotive companies.

And speaking of the "red hexagon" marque, you will find the story of the final days of the big Packards by Brooks Brierley to be of significant interest. Brooks also documents the combination of the two automotive firms of Quinby and Brooks-Ostruk.

Tracy Powell works with the automotive biography of choice in this issue and tells the fascinating career story of Art Ross. One of the great mystery cars of World War II era, dubbed the Blue Goose, is exciting concours crowds wherever it appears. Contributor George Maley shares the history and the newfound fame in keeping this interesting vehicle away from the restoration shop. In the same era, Michael L. Bromley looks at American motoring during the '40s.

Ferdinand Hediger helps us celebrate the 10 glorious years of success of Concorso Villa d'Este, and it is my pleasure to showcase the artwork of AFAS artist Dennis Brown, who captures the light spirit of motoring and motorcars with exceptional interpretative skill.

A new regular feature from Phil Berg, author of the best selling book Unique Garages, will take us into the exotic spaces of the rich and famous, and sometimes of just a super-organized car guy who knows how to take care of his magnificent machines. Finally, in keeping with the true spirit of the musical term "CODA," Bob Signom solves the riddle of James Ward Packard's pocket watch with a short, sweet-ending story.

Take your family to a motoring museum this week and drive in peace.

Gerry Durnell
Gerry Durnell
Editor & Publisher

Automobile Quarterly

The Connoisseur's Publication of Motoring
– Today, Yesterday, and Tomorrow –

GERRY DURNELL
Editor & Publisher

KAYE BOWLES-DURNELL
Associate Publisher

JOHN C. DURNELL
Chief Operations Officer, Technical Editor

TRACY POWELL
Managing Editor

JOHN EVANS
Chief Financial Officer

DAN BULLEIT
Art Director

ROD HOTTLE
Administrative Assistant

L. SCOTT BAILEY
Founding Editor and Publisher

Contributing Photographers
PHIL BERG
PATRICK ERTEL
SUZANNE STEVENS
MICHEL ZUMBRUNN

Contributing Writers
PHIL BERG
BROOKS T. BRIERLEY
MICHAEL L. BROMLEY
GAVIN FARMER
FERDINAND HEDIGER
GEORGE MALEY
RICHARD S. MANDEL
www.autoquarterly.com

ISBN 1-59613-050-4
(978-1-59613-050-0)

Printed in Korea

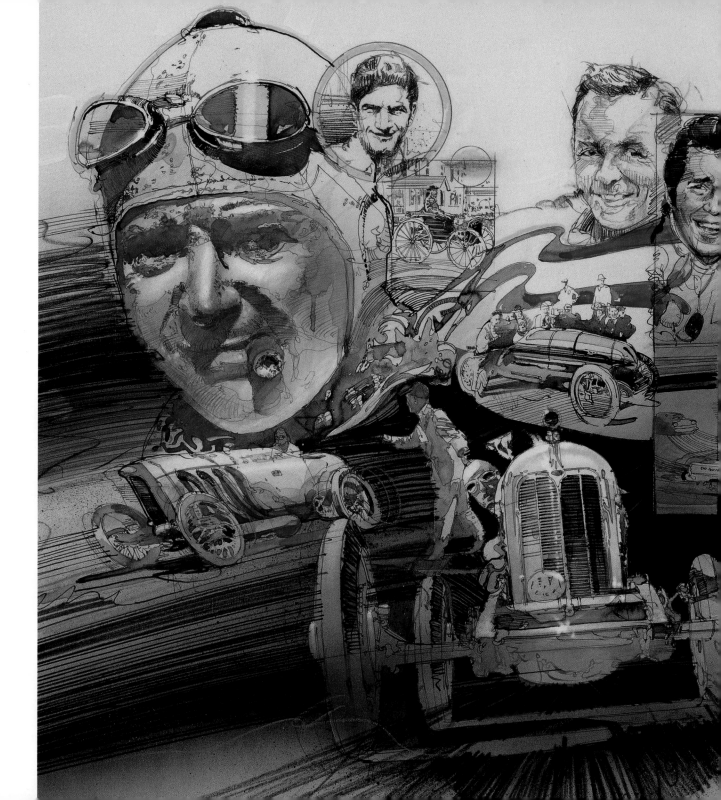

Contents

VOLUME 46, NUMBER 2 • SECOND QUARTER 2006

Cover: "Delage Interior" 17 x 21 inches, acrylic

Left: A painting for Road & Track: "100 Years of American Racing" 16 x 27 inches, acrylic

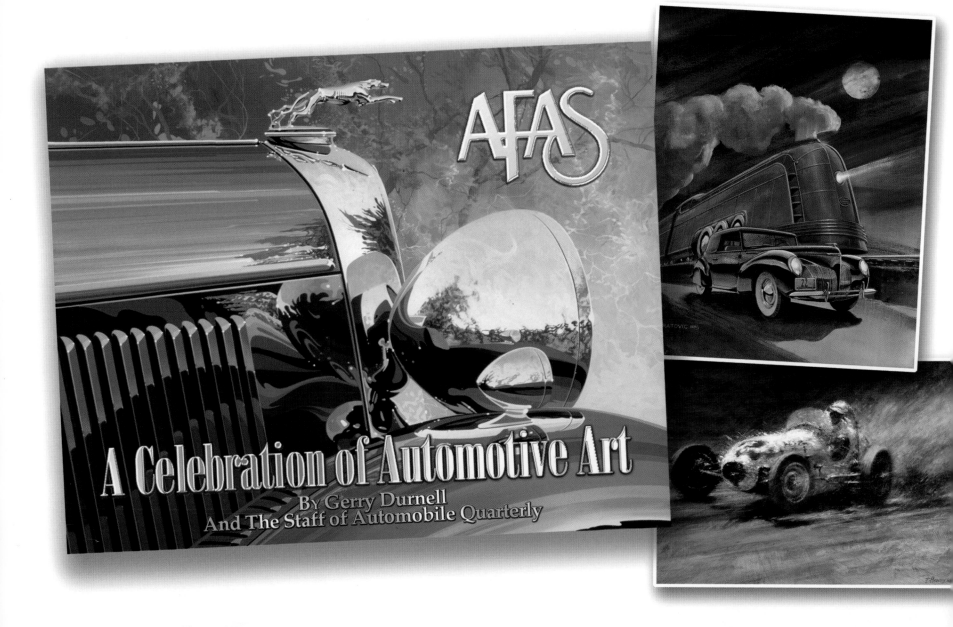

A Celebration of Automotive Art

C ome meet the world's top echelon of automotive artists in *Automobile Quarterly's* newest book, *A Celebration of Automotive Art*, a masterful compendium of the fine art and artists of the Automotive Fine Arts Society (AFAS). Articles capturing the unique personalities of all 32 artists of the AFAS are complemented by striking reproductions of their work, including the latest paintings and sculptures.

Step into the world of artistic elegance and top-shelf talent, where behind-the-canvas interviews reveal artists' impressions and philosophies. See for yourself what makes these masters tick, what stirs the passion that translates into powerful expression. This ultimate coffee-table book also covers the work and biographies of deceased automotive art luminaries such as Peter Helck, Walter Gotschke and Carlo Demand.

Lincoln Motor Car Co. announced the book's release at the 2005 Pebble Beach Concours d'Elegance, marking the 10-year anniversary of Lincoln sponsorship of AFAS at the event, and the Society's 20th Anniversary. Order your copy of *A Celebration of Automotive Art* today.

Specifications:

AFAS-A Celebration of Automotive Art
ISBN 1-59613-005-9 374 pages

$125 + s&h (PER COPY: 7-day UPS $30; 2-day UPS $60. Call for additional Canada and International charges.)

Order Today: Toll Free Phone (866) 838-2886 • Fax (812) 948-2816
Outside the U.S., call direct (812) 948-2886 • Order on our secure Web site: www.autoquarterly.com

The
Life

1A 209995

Extraordinary of the Blue Goose

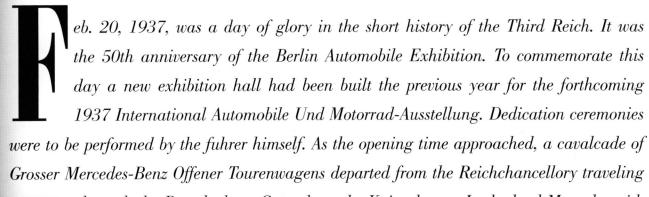

F eb. 20, 1937, was a day of glory in the short history of the Third Reich. It was the 50th anniversary of the Berlin Automobile Exhibition. To commemorate this day a new exhibition hall had been built the previous year for the forthcoming 1937 International Automobile Und Motorrad-Ausstellung. Dedication ceremonies were to be performed by the fuhrer himself. As the opening time approached, a cavalcade of Grosser Mercedes-Benz Offener Tourenwagens departed from the Reichchancellory traveling through the Brandenburg Gate along the Kaiserdamm. In the lead Mercedes with the top and all the windows down sat Adolf Hitler in the right rear seat. To his immediate left sat Hermann Goering, reichsmarschall of the Greater German Reich, president of the German Parliament (Reichstag), commander of the German Air Force (Luftwaffe) and president of the Prussian Council of State.

BY GEORGE MALEY

As the cavalcade stopped at Hall No. 1, the Waffen SS adjutant riding in the front passenger seat smartly exited the Mercedes and opened the right rear door for Hitler and his first deputy. As the party gathered around Hitler, the signal was given for the ceremonies to begin. The band started to play as Hitler walked to the podium of the new hall where he was introduced with great applause. In his speech he spoke as if the world were his audience. Hitler said, "By the cutting of the ceremonial ribbon, Germany is again reclaiming its rightful position as an industrial might to be reckoned with in the years to come."

The tour of the exhibition halls then commenced. All the notables of the German automobile industry, including Director Wilhelm Kissel of Daimler Benz, A.G., were present. It was during the tour of the Mercedes-Benz 540K exhibit that Goering spotted again a Special Roadster, which he had previously ordered in the 500K series in 1935. The 1937 Mercedes-Benz had the rear spare tire enclosed with a streamline metallic tire cover. Goering stopped

The 1937 Mercedes-Benz 540K Special Roadster at Schorfheide, near Berlin, June 3, 1939 (above and below). Goering about to enter the "Blue Goose" six years before it had acquired this nickname.

and inquired how long it might take to build this Special Roadster with the larger 5.4-liter engine with more horsepower, but with certain unusual modifications. He wanted his new Special Roadster bulletproof and bomb-resistive. He also wanted to enhance the driving range necessitating greater fuel capacity. Kissel agreed that these additions could be accomplished by the craftsmen at the Sindelfingen plant where the Special Roadster would be built.

Goering opened the driver's door and attempted to sit behind the steering wheel. He immediately encountered a problem, which he also had with his present 500K

Special Roadster. His ever-increasing waistline encroached upon the lower portion of the steering wheel.

Director Kissel, seeing Goering's dilemma, turned to his assistant in charge of the 540K custom creations. After some discussion it was decided that the entire driver's compartment could be enlarged primarily lengthwise. Assurance was given to the Reichsmarschall that Daimler Benz could make whatever changes he desired. Detailed specifications would be given to him after the design team drew up a new set of plans. Lastly Goering said that his Special Roadster had to be painted in Aviation Blue, a metallic sky-blue color as was on his present 500K Mercedes Special Roadster.

To accommodate the 220-pound Goering, the design team at the Sindelfingen plant increased the length of the driver's compartment in two ways. First, the radiator of the new Goering Special Roadster was not set back six inches compared to the normal Special Roadster. Second, to balance the new styling of the automobile with these changes, the Sindelfingen design team shortened the rear body overhang by eliminating the rear fender reverse sweep at the end of body. This overall change did not significantly detract from the beauty of the conventional design. The team also widened the width of the driver's compartment by four inches.

To accommodate a larger fuel supply, the auxiliary fuel tank on the inside of the firewall was enlarged across the whole width of the cowl. From Goering's previous aviation days' experience of World War I, he had an aircraft-type, hand-powered fuel pump placed on the floor of the Mercedes next to the emergency brake. When the driver activated this pump it forced a flow of fuel from the gasoline tank to the elevated auxiliary fuel tank on the upper portion of the cowl.

An electric sending unit under the dash could give a reading of the fuel level in each fuel tank. In case of a breakdown of the engine's mechanical fuel pump, a valve under the dash could be switched on for gasoline to flow from the auxiliary tank position by gravity to the carburetor.

The Reichsmarschall had requested that maximum protection from bullets and land mines be given to the occupants in his new Special Roadster. All the glass was made of special five-layer laminated glass of 20 mm thickness. Inside of each door was a high-strength, thin sheet of steel, which was bolted to the inside of the door panel. Also, a steel plate was attached to the inside of the cowl, while underneath the chassis a partially louvered steel plate ran the length of the car from the engine to the end of the driver's compartment. The front section of the plate was louvered, allowing heat dissipation from the

engine. A vertical steel plate was also placed behind the driver's compartment, which could be raised by a hand crank to give protection from bullets being fired from the rear of the automobile. In essence, every square inch of the inside of the driver's compartment was shielded by thin, high-tensile-strength steel plates, even including the underside of the cowl air vents.

The only change in appearance from these life protection measures was the increased height of the windshield and the door glass. In addition, the door glass was fixed in position and could not be lowered into the doors.

Goering, inspecting his new creation at the Caracciaola Mercedes-Benz Agency in Berlin in mid-July 1937, was ecstatic. (Rudy Caracciola was the lead Mercedes-Benz Grand Prix race driver during the 1930s.) The color of the metallic Aviation Blue was stunning. Goering with his own motorcycle escort had to test-drive his new exotic toy to feel the

Above: After 1958 under Dr. Bitgood's ownership, the car included the addition of swastika emblems, and had been painted black. Above right: Author George Maley next to the car's steel-plated underpinning.

increased power of the 540K supercharged engine developing 180 horsepower. On to the autobahn with his left-hand, blue-lens spotlight glowing, he engaged the screaming supercharger to reach near 160 km per hour. Returning to the Mercedes-Benz agency, he declared to Caracciola and the Mercedes-Benz design-team representative that his new Mercedes was a resounding success.

During the winter of 1940-41, Goering had the Special Roadster sent back to Daimler Benz A.G.'s Sindelfingen plant for a repaint. The metallic light blue paint had faded and had become quite dull. The technology worldwide on metallic paints in the late 1930s was still in its infancy. He had the Special Roadster repainted a darker blue with less metallic additive upon the advice of the Mercedes-Benz design department.

Goering's increasing weight (now in excess of 260 pounds) was still causing him a problem with his stomach catching the lower part of the steering wheel. The tension of the war and the lack of success of the air war in the Battle of Britain led to his disfavor with Hitler; Goering compensated with gluttony. The lack of room for his stomach was remedied by reducing the thickness of the driver's rear seat cushion by four inches. The whole back cushion was re-made with new leather. The color and the workmanship of the new leather varied slightly from the passenger-seat leather. Satisfied nevertheless with the modifications, Goering had the Special Roadster sent to his country home in Berchtesgaden, Germany, in the Obersalzberg area at the base of the Alps, where it stayed for the duration of the war.

THE CAPTURE OF THE MERCEDES-BENZ 540K SPECIAL ROADSTER

Captain Joe Crilley of the 326 Engineering Company of the 101st Airborne Division of the U.S. Army approached the picturesque town of Berchtesgaden with his unit on May 4, 1945. Crilley knew the war was coming to an end following the suicide of Hitler the previous Monday. Crilley had successfully maneuvered his company through the village with no encounter with German forces. However, the lack of a firefight did not mean that the Nazi elite were not holed up in the Eagle's Nest retreat.

This 1937 Mercedes-Benz 540K Special Roadster was liberated by the US. Army, 101st Airborne Division, at Berchtesgarden, Germany. The soldiers nicknamed the car the "Blue Goose." The photograph was taken May 4, 1945, at Berchtesgarden by Captain Joe Crilley, C Company, 326th Engineers, 101st Airborne Division (Screaming Eagles).

Crilley knew that the area surrounding the Eagle's Nest could be heavily fortified with Hitler's personal guard of Waffen SS storm troopers. As Crilley's engineering company approached the demolished homes of the Nazi elite, no evidence of enemy troops was sighted. Near the homes stood the undamaged Waffen SS housing compound and its adjacent garage.

Crilley ordered his company to spread out, but no enemy was sighted. The garage was surrounded and then entered by American troops. Inside were two magnificent Mercedes Benz automobiles side by side on the brick floor. Both cars appeared in good condition.

Crilley turned to Staff Sergeant Robert Smiley and said, "Check them out." The first of the two cars was the Goering 540K Special Roadster. The other car was a black Grosser Mercedes Offener Tourenwagon.

Smiley approached the Special Roadster with a degree of caution. He knew the Germans were notorious for setting booby traps. Taking no chances, he took aim at the driver's window in the up position and fired his weapon. Then he fired a second time leaving a .45-caliber hole in the left fender. The first bullet did not penetrate the bulletproof glass, but it left a large starburst. To the relief of Smiley, firing on the Goering Special Roadster did not spring a trap. Smiley then surveyed the Grosser Mercedes. Going

The Blue Goose, photographed in or near Berchtesgarden, Germany, between May and August 1945. The Blue Goose replaced Major General Maxwell D. Taylor's Jeep while he was in Germany. According to a report on the car when it arrived in the United States in October 1945, the color was "robin egg blue."

This photograph released in October 1945 of the two 101st Airborne Mercedes. "Touring the United States for the Victory Loan Drive". Driven by men of the 101st who found and liberated the vehicles in Berchtesgarden, Germany. The "Blue Goose" is to the right.

back to the Special Roadster, to his amazement, he found the keys in its ignition. Crilley then barked out a command: "See if it runs." After a few unsuccessful attempts, the Mercedes roared to life with a heavy growl coming from the exhaust pipe. The liberation of the Goering Special Roadster was now complete.

Several days later, Crilley and his men climbed up to the Eagle's Nest. To his surprise, he found that his unit was not the first of the Allies to reach the place; a small detachment of French and Moroccan forces had entered through the village from another direction, as the Americans were simultaneously entering the village.

Orders then came to secure the area and hold up their advance. On the day that Crilley had captured the two prized Mercedes, the German High Command started surrendering their forces. At 2:41 a.m. on May 7, 1945, the war in Europe was over.

In Berchtesgaden, Captain Crilley's 326 Engineering Company received the news with profound relief. With time on their hands, they made an exploration of the Fuhrer's retreat. The enterprising 101st Airborne soldiers found a cachet of French Cognac and choice French wines in the basement of the garage.

Before long the two Mercedes, after being cleaned by their new "owners," were being driven all over the village of Berchtesgaden by the 101st Airborne celebrating the end of the war in Europe. The soldiers' exploits soon reached higher-ups. Word soon came from General Ryan, the sector commander, for the two Mercedes to be parked. When Major General Maxwell Taylor, overall theater commander, saw the "Hitler" 540K Special Roadster a few days later, he thought it would make a great command car. He then turned to his adjutant and said, "Put my two-star license plate on the Blue Goose," the name the Americans had given to the automobile.

The command car status did not last long for General Taylor. In August, he received orders of reassignment as the new superintendent of West Point Military Academy. At the same time, word was received from the U.S. Treasury Department that these two prized possessions of Hitler's would be a great draw in war-bond rallies back home. Crilley was requested to tour the United States with the two Mercedes along with his soldiers. He turned the assignment down; Crilley had another agenda and it was getting out of the Army as soon as possible and coming back home and getting married. But Second Lieutenant James Cox, who served in Crilley's outfit, had fallen in love with the Special Roadster. Cox volunteered for the special assignment. Actually Cox had tried to buy the Blue Goose from American authorities. But the Army denied the purchase request, seeing that the greater good was a war-bond tour.

THE BLUE GOOSE COMES TO THE UNITED STATES

The Special Roadster and the Mercedes-Benz Grosser 770 Offener Tourenwagon received a shipping order issued on Sept. 10, 1945, by the Headquarters U.S. Forces, European Theater indicating that these two automobile war trophies would be sent to the states accompanied by a contingent from the 101st Airborne Division of 10 men and Lieutenant James Cox in charge. Although the original thinking was that these two Mercedes belonged to Hitler, it was later determined that the Special Roadster belonged to Hermann Goering, as it sported a crest of his coat of arms on the doors. Hitler did not use a coat of arms. Subsequent supporting purchase documents verified this conclusion.

The war-bond tour was to start on Nov. 2, 1945, from Washington, D.C., traveling west to four cities in Pennsylvania, 10 cities in Ohio and three cities in Indiana. After a period of 45 days, the group was to return to Washington for further assignments. A second tour was made through Illinois and Nebraska in early 1946.

In August 1946, the first reunion of the 101st

The car was shipped to the United States to participate in a war bond tour, which began in November 1945. It was joined by the other Mercedes-Benz found at the Eagle's Nest, the Grosser 770 Offener Tourenwagon.

Airborne Division was held in Indianapolis with the Blue Goose on hand for the reunion. Anton (Tony) Hulman, owner of the Indianapolis Motor Speedway, invited the 101st Airborne Division to bring the Blue Goose to the track pacing two special trophy races of three cars each. Hulman drove the Blue Goose around the famous track leading the three Indy race cars to a flying start. Major General Maxwell Taylor was on hand to view his old command car. With the war over the Blue Goose was retired from active war-bond rallies and placed in storage.

The Goering Special Roadster ended up as surplus government property in 1956, and was auctioned off by the Property Disposal Branch, Logistics Division, Aberdeen Proving Ground in Maryland. An auction was held of the two Mercedes on Oct. 5, 1956. The bid description read, "MERCEDES-BENZ Convertible Roadster (Several informational sources indicate that this car was the private sporty car of Hermann Goering and have identified the heraldic design on the doors as Goering's assumed coat-of-arms.) Acq. Cost Unknown. USED." The high bid was $2,167; it was awarded to Jacques Tunick of Greenwich, Conn.

Upon capture at the Eagle's Nest, Staff Sergeant Robert Smiley fired his .45 caliber at the Blue Goose to spring any potential booby trap, leaving bullet holes in the windshield and the left fender.

The dashboard: A—Oil pressure gauge; B—Choke; C—Tachometer; D—Switches for left, right traffic signals; E—Oil, gas indicators; F—Starter button; G—Speedometer; H—Throttle; I—Dummy dial; J—Radio, glove compartment; K—Horn; L—Fuel pump; M—Hand brake; N—Gear shift; O—Ventilators; P—Cigar lighter. The Mercedes-Benz has four speeds forward.

DOLF SCHICKELGRUBER'S (alias Hitler) super-de luxe Mercedes-Benz nvertible coupe, minus, of course, "Der efirer," arrived in Dayton last week the interests of the current "Victory oan" campaign.

Though quite few persons ere able to get

HITLER'S HACK

THE BITGOOD ERA OF THE BLUE GOOSE

The purchase of the Blue Goose by Dr. George Bitgood Jr. from Jacques Tunick in 1958 had to a degree been pre-ordained in an unspoken meeting between Bitgood, a sea merchantman, and the future deputy reichsfuhrer of Germany, Hermann Goering, in a chance encounter in a tavern in Stockholm, Sweden. Bitgood, who always had a love of the sea, joined the United States Merchant Marine in his late teens, contrary to the wishes of his father and uncle, who were noted veterinarians in the New England area. They wanted George to follow in their footsteps.

It was early 1922, while sailing the Trans Atlantic route, when his ship docked in Stockholm. While on shore leave he went to a local tavern where he found

It was first thought that both cars discovered at the Eagle's Nest were those of Adolf Hitler's, as evidenced in newspaper accounts and this war bond tour photo.

a large crowd gathered around a German-speaking man "holding court" with many admirers. It was Goering, who had become the last air ace to command the von Richthofen Squadron in July 1918. The legendary air ace, Manfred von Richthofen, known and feared by the Allied Forces as the "Red Baron," was killed in action earlier that year. Bitgood was fascinated by the persona of Goering. He felt a reluctance to speak

to him because of the language barrier. As he was about to leave the tavern, he couldn't resist going over to the corner where Goering was entertaining his court of admirers to get a closer look. Bitgood caught Goering's eye and for just a few split seconds Goering smiled back at the young American. That moment in time would leave a lasting impression

upon Bitgood, leading him eventually to purchase the Blue Goose from Tunick for $10,000.

Leaving the service of the Merchant Marines in 1930, Bitgood eventually did follow in his father's and uncle's footsteps and entered Ontario Veterinarian College at the University of Toronto in 1931. Following graduation, he set up practice in Middletown, Conn., and practiced for 61 years.

Although dedicated to veterinarian medicine, he slowly acquired an interest in exotic cars in a very private way. In the 1940s, Bitgood started a hobby of buying, selling and trading automotive classics. In 1949, he purchased Jack Warner's (of Warner Brothers Movie Studios) 1937 Mercedes-Benz 540K Special Roadster from Dr. Sam Scher, a noted plastic surgeon with offices on Park Avenue in New York City. Then he acquired the Blue Goose.

Once Bitgood turned his attention to the Mercedes-Benz 500K and 540K series, he left the hobby as a trader and seller, turning his attention as an accumulator of these prized Mercedes models. Over the years, his prewar Mercedes-Benz collection reached 14, of which four were Special Roadsters.

Bitgood, upon acquiring the Goering Special Roadster, had it repainted black. Some of the chrome pieces were re-chromed. Where Goering had his coat-of-arms painted on each door, Bitgood had the doors painted over. He had two brass plates fabricated with engraved swastikas and had each attached to a door. He also had the original blue carpet replaced with nylon looped carpeting, which was popular at that time. However, he did not have the bullet hole repaired in the fender nor did he replace the damaged glass in the left driver's window.

In early 1974, Bitgood contacted the 101st Airborne Division located in Fort Campbell, Ky., concerning bringing the Blue Goose to a reunion. But the reunion

Above: The 2002 gathering of 101st Airborne Division troops and the Blue Goose. Right: Present-day owners wisely chose to preserve the car in its unique, storied state.

was never realized, because Bitgood was diagnosed with kidney cancer and fell ill.

In 1993, Bitgood, now 88, decided to sell his collection. He turned to Herbert von Fragstein, of Dayton, Ohio, whom he had known for several years as a noted private collector of prewar classic Mercedes-Benzes. Although von Fragstein did not display a direct interest in buying any individual Mercedes in the Bitgood collection, he showed an interest in helping Bitgood sell the collection.

Bitgood died in 1998. Following his death, Bitgood's son-in-law, Jim Champion, who is married to the executor of his estate, went to Dayton to secure Bitgood's unsold Mercedes-Benzes from von Fragstein. However, von Fragstein refused to release them. The case went to court in Montgomery County (Dayton) in 1998. After a lengthy and costly court battle with von Fragstein, the court granted the Bitgood Trust possession of the cars. At the conclusion of the legal proceedings, Champion asked Chris Charlton of Classic Car Services of Oxford, Maine, to prepare the car for sale. The work performed was to put the automobile in good running condition.

When Bitgood's daughters heard that the 101st Airborne Division was planning to build a new museum at Fort Campbell, they were eager to fulfill their father's dream of a reunion of the Blue Goose with the remaining veterans of World War II and present troops of the 101st Airborne Division. The initial reunion envisioned by Bitgood took place in June 2002. Champion attended the reunion. After the event the Blue Goose was transported to the Champion's home in California.

Before the Blue Goose was publicly shown, a buyer was found that would fit the unique desire of preserving the automobile in all of its historical significance—Carnlough International Limited of Guernsey, Great Britain.

As part of its assets, Carnlough maintains a unique but small collection of highly valued automobiles. For the past five years, Carnlough had been seeking an authentic but un-restored Mercedes-Benz Special Roadster. When the principals laid their eyes on the Goering Mercedes, a deal was shortly struck with the Bitgood estate. Upon the recommendation of Champion, Classic Auto Services was contacted again to bring the Goering Special Roadster back to the condition when it was first found by the 101st Airborne Division on May 4, 1945.

THE PRESERVATION/RESTORATION OF HERMANN GOERING'S MERCEDES-BENZ 540K SPECIAL ROADSTER

In many respects a preservation/restoration of a classic car 65 years of age is much different than a body-off restoration, which creates the illusion of a showroom-condition automobile. The instructions from the Carnlough International Limited Trust were to recreate the Special Roadster as it was when the American soldiers took custody of it. At that time, the Goering automobile was 8

years old. It had been maintained over the years in excellent condition; however, it was not showroom quality. The Trust wanted the .45-caliber hole in the left fender as well as the large star in the left-door window glass to be left intact. Many chrome pieces, which had been re-plated by Bitgood, had been crudely prepared thus necessitating re-chroming. Because of modern chemicals, today's chrome creates a brighter luster than chrome work done in the late 1930s. To bring a consistency of brightness to the old chrome, a dulling agent was added to the chrome bath. As to the engine and its immediate accessory systems such as the distributor, only cleaning agents were applied. These cleaning agents were also applied to the engine block. Then a thin agent of oil was applied. This oiling process has to be renewed yearly; otherwise, a thin coat of rust will start to build up on the engine block.

As the paint was being removed from the body, the restorers found that there were two different colors of blue paint which had been applied during Goering's ownership. Several paint samples were made for the principals of the Trust. Since Lieutenant Cox had died, contact was made with Crilley. Crilley has been a most successful artist since his return from active

The Blue Goose in 2005. Note that the number plate is, in fact, incorrect: Goering's actual number plate was "IA 209995"— the "IA" is for Berlin. Top: The commemorative plaque from the car's "rescuers."

military service in 1946. His paint selection was then agreed upon by the two principals of the Trust.

The leather of the seats and side panels was saved by washing and then applying softening agents. Where the leather had cracked on the seats, a muslin underlay was laminated on the backside of the original leather. The stitching, where the leather pieces of the seat and back cushions were joined, was meticulously removed and then re-stitched. The springs of the seats and cushions were all rebuilt. Where the horsehair padding had deteriorated, new horsehair was added.

Above: Captain Joe Crilley again meets the Blue Goose in 2004 to confirm the paint color from his recollections. **Right:** The leather rumble seats were missing and had to be replaced.

Leather seats in the rumble seat area were missing and had to be made. But the new seats had to be brought into conformity with the driver compartment seat's leather. To accomplish this task, the new leather was distressed to make it look aged and used.

Classic Auto Services had to seek items that had been taken off the car by American souvenir hunters. The cigar lighter was missing as was the ashtray and the clock. Where the clock should have been mounted there was a temperature gauge.

Certain engine accessories were chrome-plated, namely the horn inside the engine compartment as well as the two tie bars from the radiator to the cowl. Were these pieces chromed by Bitgood or were they painted? After much research a decision was made that the chrome was original to the Special Roadster.

The carpet was replaced. A good section of the original material was found behind the driver compartment seats. In spots the carpet had faded. It had been a fine woolen pile and blue in color. A matching material was purchased and made to fit the Special Roadster. For several weeks the new floor covering was laid out on the shop floor and walked on to give it an aged look.

As the Mercedes came back together, modern paint had to be given a dulling agent to give a somewhat aged look to the paint. The newly re-chromed pieces all match the original chrome. The outer radiator shell had several minor blemishes as did the other minor chrome pieces, but it was still in excellent condition. Charlton had to decide on each piece, whether to restore it to a modified condition or to retain it in its original condition. A consistency of age and quality of all parts, in harmony one to the other, is the qualifying factor of a preservation/restoration project. Since this was not a body-off preservation/restoration, the Blue Goose is probably the most original 540K Special Roadster in existence today.

EPILOGUE

When Goering's Mercedes-Benz 540K Special Roadster is shown at various concours in times to come, people no doubt will marvel at the car and its lineage. More important, many will recognize the automobile as a vital piece of history, during which Europe was liberated in part by the blood of American troops.

The Goering roadster is a historical contradiction in values. It has remarkable finish not seemingly overdone. It appears to be a hands-on car ready to move out without fear of being soiled. One can visualize Major General Maxwell Taylor driving around Germany in this beauty in contrast to the very few cars on the roads at the end of World War II. But the bigger contradiction is the damage done to the Special Roadster by the 101st Airborne Division when it was captured. Onlookers will no doubt ask about the bullet hole in the fender and the bullet star in the driver's side window glass. Many will wonder why subsequent owners never had the Special Roadster returned to the Goering original ownership condition. Moving a historical piece out of a wartime setting to a concours field where perfection is the norm will no doubt befuddle many an onlooker.

It is the intent and wish of the present owners that today's generation might have a greater appreciation of the cost and sacrifice of war after viewing the Blue Goose. **AO**

After a painstaking restoration by Classic Auto Services, the Blue Goose lives on under the ownwership of Carnlough International Limited of Guernsey, Great Britian.

Art Gallery with Dennis Brown

Dennis Brown can tell you about the "California scene." He's lived it—literally. Born in 1944 in Los Angeles, Brown attended elementary and secondary schools there, then majored in fine arts at California State College at Long Beach. Afterwards he took night classes in illustration at Otis-Parsons Art Institute. He still lives in the Golden State, in Covina. It's no surprise, then, that the region's renown for automotive customization is part of him, and he a part of it. He's more likely to have either a camera or a brush in his hands, however, than a wrench.

BY TRACY POWELL

"Day of the Woodie" 14 ½ x 15 inches, acrylic.

rown's life and career is just as customized as one of the '34 Ford three-window coupes he helped friends build in high school.

"We used to build the cars," said Brown. "We didn't buy them from the factory. I've always loved cars, loved going to car shows as a little boy. Dad would take me, and I was so insane over them and I would go home and draw."

The allure was "the beauty of the styling of the cars, and the body parts. I was more interested in the outside of the car, the shape of the fenders, and how it would swoop back. I'm keen on that until today."

Brown knew he wanted to be an illustrator or an artist as early as his elementary school years, an early inspiration coming from the works of Norman Rockwell. By seventh and eighth grades, the bud-

ding artist was winning awards from various sources, including citywide contests and one from Hallmark Cards.

"They were illustrations," said Brown, "of the future of America, a montage of all different things at that time that were important to me, like space exploration and education … this was the beginning of the space race."

Later, as a college graduate and while attending Otis-Parsons, technical design became important to Brown. During this time, he worked with a crew of machinists and mechanics at Schiefer Engineering, cranking out hot-rod speed equipment designed and manufactured by Paul Schiefer.

For the next 10 years, Brown was immersed in the architecture field.

The artist in his Covina, Calif. studio.

"I learned perspective and everything else in architecture; use of colors for interiors and the line work. We did everything in line work. It was a delineator for the architects. An architect would draw a set of plans—floor plans and elevation—and we would make them three-dimensional."

Dabbling in auto art was sprinkled throughout this period. Some of Brown's drawings appeared in *Road & Track* in 1977. "That's how most people saw my work."

Brown's style emerged from these early black-and-white, pen-and-ink illustrations, evolving into what soon became a unique, striking style. The result is vivid, deep-layered colors with hot high-

"Sunday Drive in Tuscany" 28 x 34 inches, acrylic.

lights, which, as Dean Batchelor once noted, bring out colors glistening so much that the car looks freshly painted and still wet from the spray gun. "His approach to his subjects is as fresh as the look he gives them, displaying intense color and vitality," continued Batchelor. "Dennis is a master at diminishing color values; the front of the car in perspective brighter and more defined than the part that's in the background."

As Brown explains, the overall effect is intended to convey an unfiltered perception to the observer. "I love to have people see what I can see. That's the only way I can convey that. I'm not a great writer, so I use artwork to show how I see automobiles. My stuff is super transparent; you can see right down to the lines.

"When I do my oils, I do the 'ink thing' [outlining in pen and ink] and then paint on top with oils. I get a great deal of luminescence. That's what I see, and I try to bring that across."

Brown also gets results by using "liquid acrylics over line work, then going back and splashing acrylic gouache over it." Composition almost constantly vies with subject matter in the mind of Dennis Brown. "Sure, it's a passion. I have all these things floating in my head that I want to do."

For this artist, mixing up the subject matter, and having fun at it, is a must, "otherwise it would become stale. Not all cars, but landscapes and birds and flowers and portraits."

He also does food illustration for Westways magazine, and conceptual drawing for Universal Studios. "When they're building new amusement parks, I'll do miniature sketches so they can see what the rides are like. That's really fun—they take you to Universal Studios, and show you how all these things work.

"I have to do that other stuff to get my mind away and charge it up."

Once charged and back painting automotive, his hands-down druthers: Ferrari, and all the marque's trappings.

"Summer Fan" 23 x 17 inches, acrylic.

Left: "Summer Getaway" 32 x 34 inches, acrylic. Above: "TR No. 46" 12 x 34 inches. Below: "HMW Stovebolt Special" 24 x 26, acrylic.

"I like Ferraris of all years," said Brown," especially open-wheeled roadsters. Once a year I go to West Palm Beach to the Cavallino Ferrari show. Usually the people who are at those shows are billionaires, and they have these beautiful collections, these cars. There's the styling of Pininfarina, Bertone. That styling is wonderful stuff. The way they do it makes it beautiful, even the dashboards in some. When they put it together, it always looks so classy, on the inside as well, with all the piping and the stitching."

But it's more than the styling. "Here's where I love the mechanics; the sound of that car's 12-cylinder engine is a sound to be heard."

This explains his leaning toward painting legendary racing drivers, like Fangio. "We can get photographs of this guy now. Most of my paintings are from events, historical races. Old drivers are really fun to paint. But you have to be careful not to use someone's photograph to the T."

The self-described "quiet one" of the founding members of AFAS, Brown teaches at a local college from 8 a.m. to noon. He is normally working

on three to four projects, which include commissions like the 2003 poster for the "Eyes On Design" auto design exhibition. All this comprises the bulk of Brown's customized career, which continues to garner awards. In 2004 he won the AFAS Athena Award of Excellence, and most recently he received accolades from a sweeping contest sponsored by the magazine International Artist involving thousands of artists from around the globe.

"It keeps you young, and looking around, and doing things. It keeps you interested in life. I don't think any of us are really going to retire, and even if we could we'd go crazy if we just sat down."

Above: "250 GT SWB" 20 x 30 inches, acrylic.
Right: Eyes on Design Poster, 30 x 40 inches, acrylic.
Opposite: "1932 Chrysler Imperial" 27 x 35 inches, acrylic.

Giugiaro's Bugattis

> "As a car designer, Bugattis have always held a fascination for me and I have always wanted to design one."
>
> Giorgetto Giugiaro

There is a mystical lure about the name Bugatti that is virtually irresistible. Most people think of it as a French name; after all, Ettore Bugatti built his cars in the grounds of his beautiful Chateau Saint Jean, near Molsheim on the Alsace region a little to the west of Strasbourg, a former German city built on the banks of the Rhine. Ettore used the chateau as a place where he could present his new creations to the world, as well as a place for entertainment of special guests.

He also raced his cars on the race tracks of Europe in the colors of France after the Saar region was ceded to France in 1919.

But the fact remains that by birth Ettore Bugatti was Italian, and in recent times other Italians have tried to revive his legend. That they were unsuccessful is immaterial to this story.

BY GAVIN FARMER

The road to revival of the famous Bugatti name and the involvement of Giorgetto Giugiaro has many twists and turns and involves a wide range of characters. In the beginning, some time in the mid-1980s, there were three main players: Ferruccio Lamborghini, Jean-Marc Borel and Romano Artioli. Lamborghini, who was in retirement, needs no introduction having already created his own brand of supercars; enthusiasts of the marque would know the name Borel as the author of some books on Lamborghini and his cars. Borel's daytime occupation was director of a French finance company. Romano Artioli was the unknown at that

time and was introduced to Lamborghini and Borel through an ex-Lamborghini employee. Artioli was at the time possibly the world's largest Ferrari dealer with dealerships in northern Italy and southern Germany; he was also a major Suzuki distributor. He was wealthy, he was a car nut, and when he heard about the ideas the others were kicking around—namely to revive the name Bugatti with a state-of-the-art supercar—he immediately wanted in.

It took some time and a great deal of negotiating—and money—to secure the rights to the Bugatti name, but by October 1987 Borel had registered Bugatti Automobili in Modena. To run the new

enterprise and direct the engineering of the new car, ex-Lamborghini engineer Paolo Stanzani was recruited along with several colleagues who had been operating a consultancy. A site was selected to build a spectacular factory in the Emilian town of Campogalliano, a few kilometers out of Modena. Work on the site began in early 1988 with early layouts of the proposed new car beginning at around the same time.

It was to be a car at the leading edge of technology. Its specification seemed surreal at the time: all-alloy, midship, 3.5-liter dohc V12 engine with four turbochargers driving all four wheels through an

Giorgetto Giugiaro's first Bugatti design in his long illustrious career was the ID90. Apart from the Bugatti badge on the nose, however, it was perhaps little more than another mid-engined supercar proposal.

in-house designed and built transmission system. Considerable input was sought from specialists in carbon fiber technology, aerodynamics and tires.

Artioli asked renowned freelance stylist Marcello Gandini—he had an enviable CV in designing supercars, the Lamborghini Diablo being among his designs—to design the new car's body, a process that evolved through 1989 and into 1990. He never completed the design of the EB110 and the end result is a little challenging aesthetically, according to critics.

Giugiaro was well aware of the activities at Campogalliano and was looking for an opportunity to design his version of what the forthcoming Bugatti could look like. A set of engineering drawings was provided by Artioli and in mid-1989 Giugiaro sat at his drawing board and sketched what became the ID90 concept car.

Its styling is characterized by a full glass canopy that covers the passenger compartment and flows back over the mid-mounted engine. "Steps" on either side of the canopy directs air into the engine compartment, supplementing air that channels in from the scoop low on each side. Viewed from above the canopy has a teardrop-like shape that tapers towards the rear.

Where the Gandini design is somewhat chiseled in its "wedginess," the Giugiaro design is much softer, its lines flow more readily. The rounded front with its prominent spoiler houses the headlights on either side of a large Bugatti badge, the famous horseshoe radiator conspicuous by its absence. To perhaps compensate, Giugiaro designed the ID90's alloy road wheels in the style of those from the 1926 Royale. A neat innovation was found in the doors: the lower half up to the belt line opened normally while the upper part—the glass part—was raised automatically when the lower part was activated.

Giugiaro presented the ID90 at the 1990 Turin Motor Show where it drew high praise but no commission from Bugatti Automobili. "As a car designer, Bugattis have always held a fascination for me and I have always wanted to design one," said Giugiaro. "To me, besides being sporty, a Bugatti

was a luxurious automobile with a special style. I knew that Artioli wanted a four-door model that would be sporty and practical—the EB110 was not a practical car—and since I wanted a free project for the forthcoming Geneva Salon, he provided me with the mechanical components for us to design and build a prototype on our own initiative."

The Bugatti EB112, as the big four-door saloon was badged, was the star of the Geneva Salon in 1993. It was a bold statement of automobile design as well as a blend of style icons from famous Bugattis of the past, most notably the rare Atlantic with which the EB112 shared the central spine.

Before Giugiaro began sketching what would become a masterpiece of automobile design, the Bugatti EB112, he did some background research. "I read as many books on the marque as I could, absorbing details of its history and its tradition as well as studying photographs of classic Bugattis," said Giugiaro. "I also visited several museums where I could observe their form, their shape, and I also chatted with many renowned Bugatti experts on what

they would expect a modern-day example to be."

Work began on the EB112 in September 1992, a mere nine months before its appointment in Geneva. In many respects, the layout and size of the mechanical components determined, to some extent, the style of the car. It was to be a front-engined V12 sedan driving all four wheels through a five-speed manual gearbox. The wheelbase was set at 122 inches and the overall length was to be no more than 196.8 inches. As Giugiaro said with a grin, "I missed that one by this much," holding his thumb and forefinger about two-and-a-half inches apart. Its width was to be 77 inches while the height was set at 55.3 inches.

An early decision by Giugiaro was to design the EB112 as a two-box sedan; the roofline would flow

An early sketch by Giugiaro for the EB112, a high-performance luxury limousine that carried several Bugatti styling cues.

back and down in a continuous curve to the rear bumper. Taking a cue from the famous Bugatti Atlantic, Giugiaro included a discreet rib running from the front grille over the hood, across the roof where it bisects the rear windows and down over the trunk lid to the bumper. Immediately the EB112 looks distinctively different. It has that look that sets it apart from the many big luxury sedans on the market with these two style features. Running divergently across

opens clamshell-like to reveal the engine.

As with the ID90, the EB112 features alloy wheels that resemble those from the Royale.

Giugiaro and his engineering partner Aldo Mantovani pushed the technology boundaries during the construction of the EB112, all with Artioli's blessing (he was a frequent visitor to Italdesign during the car's construction), by developing a carbon fiber tub as its chassis. This was a first for such a large automobile. Attached to the tub was a sophisticated, fully independent wishbone-and-coil-spring suspension system, and an all-aluminum body.

The interior, designed by Fabrizio Giugiaro (son of Giorgetto and Italdesign Giugiaro Styling Area Director), evokes a feeling of calm and solitude. Upholstered entirely in leather, it was designed intentionally to seat only four people in absolute comfort with no compromises whatsoever. It combines classic elegance with modern materials, with the dashboard designed to provide the driver

Above: The EB112 was a beautifully styled limousine that was even better in the metal. It was the first of Giugiaro's Bugattis to carry the horseshoe grille and a modern interpretation of the classic Royale alloy wheels. It never entered series production. Right: Giugiaro designed an interior trimmed entirely in soft rouched leather and included every luxury item then available. Despite its size, the EB112 was strictly a four-seater.

the hood from either side of the horseshoe grille are two discreet "shoulders" that cut back to the base of the A-pillar and then continue up along the edge of the roof to define the outline of the side windows that again take their cue from classic Bugattis. Rather than hide the headlights, Giugiaro opted to have them exposed, placing them in individual housings on either side of the grille.

Another interesting styling touch is the vertical vent behind the front wheel arches that assists in evacuating air from under the hood. Giugiaro: "That was not on my original proposal, it was added after a suggestion from Artioli, and I like it." The hood is a work of metal art; pressed from an aluminum sheet it with the feeling of being in a cockpit that is trimmed in briarwood around the instruments, the center console, accents along the doors and the armrests. It is not over-powering in any way, but all that an EB112 owner would expect to be there—high-quality audio system and automatic climate control, among other touches that mark the car as special—are there.

With the success of its showing at Geneva, Italdesign and Bugatti Automobili entered into a joint venture to produce the EB112 in limited numbers beginning in 1995. "We thought we could build about 300 units a year," said Giugiaro. However, it became clear by October 1994 that Bugatti was in financial trouble and so only three prototypes were ever completed, plus a number of unused components. Bugatti

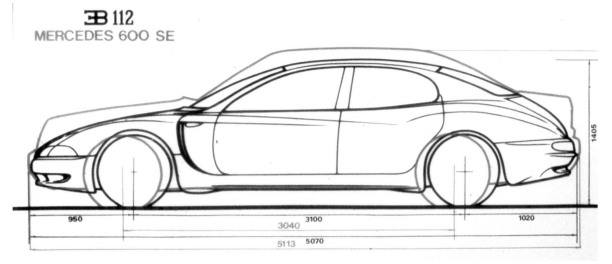

Compared with the Mercedes-Benz 600 SE, the EB112 was considerably lower and sleeker with radically different proportions.

Automobili filed for bankruptcy in September 1995 and all assets, including parts for incomplete EB112s, were auctioned off.

Only one of the three prototypes has survived, it being co-owned by Italdesign and a wealthy businessman who lives in Monaco. (All three prototypes were built and paid for by Italdesign, incidentally.)

"This car was an expensive missed opportunity for us," recalled Giugiaro with a touch of emotion in his voice. "We should have bought the cars and parts from Bugatti and built them ourselves. It just shows we do not attach enough value to what we do because those who bought the materials from the auction all made money out of it. The EB112 was a dream car which was production-ready and has remained close to our hearts ever since. It was the car I wanted for my retirement." The car was hailed as a masterpiece of automotive design that embraced all the virtues of the high-class automobile that Bugatti represented. So much so that the Italian publisher Automobilia in Milano awarded Giugiaro and the EB112 the L'Automobile più Bella del Mondo prize.

There is considerable significance in the model names for the EB110 and EB112: the digits represent the years since Ettore's birth.

In April 1998, Volkswagen AG purchased the rights to the name Bugatti. The driving force behind this decision was Ferdinand Piëch, grandson of Ferdinand Porsche, and the top executive of the vast Volkswagen empire. He and Romano Artioli met several times

in Wolfsburg during the first few weeks of 1998 before the purchase was announced to the world. Piëch was well known for his love and knowledge of motorcars as well as his commitment to the survival of important marque names. No doubt these feelings were behind the VW Group's purchase not only of Bugatti but also Bentley and Lamborghini.

Having bought the name, Piëch made the decision to build his Bugatti in Molsheim, the spiritual home of the brand. As he commented, "Ettore Bugatti started his company in 1909 in Molsheim, and there was never any doubt about continuing the Bugatti heritage and tradition at the place where the unique reputation of the marque had it roots." He was against taking over the existing (and unoccupied) Campogalliano factory because he wanted to avoid his Bugatti being labeled as another northern Italian supercar. To this end, VW has spent a considerable sum of money refurbishing Chateau Saint Jean, as well as building a facility to assemble the Bugatti 16/4 Veyron.

There is an interesting side road to the career of Piëch that involved Giorgetto Giugiaro and Italdesign. After Piëch had departed from Porsche and before he joined Audi he took what we would call a working holiday in Italy at the end of 1971 and into the early months of 1972. As Giugiaro explained, "He said he wanted to learn as much as he could about coachbuilding and to learn Italian. And, you know, he was always so punctual—he was in my office on the first day before I was." The two men became firm friends then and remain so to this day.

When Piëch assumed command of Bugatti he naturally turned to his good friend Giorgetto Giugiaro in June 1998 for ideas on what ought to carry the famous Bugatti name and badge.

An agreement was signed between the two companies for the production of three prototypes for evaluation by Volkswagen with the possibility of series production. "There were no guarantees on that and I knew that from the start," said Giugiaro, who added, "Personally I was hoping that Piëch would buy the EB112 design from me but he was adamant that 'his' Bugatti would utilize a Volkswagen engine and chassis."

From Piëch's point of view, Volkswagen had to investigate and learn about the heritage, the traditions and values of the marque. He said of this, "Time was taken to get to understand both the marque as well as the spirit of Bugatti. How was it to be positioned today, how could the traditional characteristics be projected into today's motoring environment or, in other words: how would Ettore Bugatti have designed a car at the beginning of the 21st century?"

The company accordingly sought views from Giugiaro as well as from potential clients, the media, the industry and the many Bugatti clubs around the world about a modern interpretation of a Bugatti motorcar, whether it be a coupe, limousine or sportscar.

The first fruit of the collaboration was the Bugatti EB118 that was shown at the Paris Salon in October 1998. In a three-month period of frantic activity, Giugiaro, father and son, created a completely new running model using mechanical components supplied by VW. An enormous 6.3-liter W18-cylinder 550hp engine—the first such engine type to power an automobile—driving all four wheels through an automatic gearbox, powered the EB118.

What Volkswagen, and in particular Piëch, wanted

Above: The full-sized EB118 clay model in Italdesign's studio with its creators, Fabrizio Giugiaro on the left, Giorgetto in the middle and Ferdinand Piëch on the right. Below: Many styling cues for the EB118 were carried over from the EB112, which probably counted against it in Piëch's mind.

was a two-door coupe that would be the proud bearer of the Bugatti name and badge.

Given the timeframe involved, there were a number of stylistic carry-overs from the EB112 of fond memory. The front styling is very reminiscent of the

EB112 and the delicate longitudinal rib was there, too. Interestingly, the wheelbase was longer and the bulk of its volume had been moved rearwards ever-so-slightly in retaining the coupe style that was desired by Piëch. Several times during the construction of the EB118, Piëch called at Italdesign to monitor progress and change details as he saw appropriate.

The extremely functional interior was designed by Fabrizio Giugiaro in consultation with Hartmut Warkuss, head of the Volkswagen Centre of Excellence, and Piëch. It was roomy, as required, and contained enough art deco touches to evoke memories of the thirties, yet without being overtly retro in any way.

The reaction to the Bugatti EB118—the first digit representing the first of the series, the last two digits representing the engine's cylinder count—was muted in comparison with the EB112 five years earlier. Nevertheless, it was a superb piece of automotive design work but one got the feeling that

it was not exactly what Piëch wanted as his pinnacle automobile.

Behind the scenes, Giorgetto and Fabrizio were working on the second part of Piëch's plan to reinvent the spirit of Bugatti, the EB218. This was a further development of the themes and emotions already encapsulated in the beautiful EB112 from 1993. It took the EB118's W18-cylinder engine and AWD driveline and placed it under a big limousine body. The EB218 was even longer than the EB112 at 211.6 inches as well as being slightly wider at 78.35 inches and higher at 57.3 inches. It was an imposing automobile. Like the EB112, the EB218 retained the classic Bugatti styling elements, but also established its own identity in a design that exuded grace and power.

Compared with the EB112, the styling differences were subtle but significant. Apart from the physical increase, there was a far greater use of chrome on the EB218: highlights around the side windows to emphasize a traditional Bugatti icon—the side windows often emanated from a point at the A-pillar—and a single piece low down on the doors; the air vents on the sides of the front fenders were picked out with a C-shaped chrome band; the hood was of a more conventional shape with a normal opening; the rear windscreen was a single piece of glass (not split); the headlights and taillamps were re-shaped; and the wheels had slightly different emphasis in their finish (still resembling modern-day replicas of the wheels

Like the dashboard of the EB112, that of the EB218 was large and imposing in a somewhat "retro" style.

35

from the Royale, however). Inside, Fabrizio Giugiaro had taken the theme he and Warkuss had established for the EB118 and reworked it slightly for the new environment. It was still full of Art Deco touches, was made from the best materials and was designed to accommodate four people in sybaritic comfort.

Released for display at the Geneva Salon in 1999, many observers saw the EB218 as the first vision of Bugatti by Volkswagen. It was highly praised and liked by all who saw it, although it must be said that this praise was not as effusive as that for the EB112. As good as it was, for Piëch it was not exactly what he was seeking. Perhaps a factor here was his concern that the EB218 would have been viewed as a competitor for the forthcoming Bentley range that he had signed off—the Continental GT coupe and Continental Flying Spur saloon that would be derived from it. The market in the rarefied air at the very top was capable of absorbing only so many luxury limousines no matter what the badge of honor on the grille.

Also, what was not known then was that a third member of the family was under construction at

Above: The Bugatti EB218 was long, large and luxurious in every way and was quite possibly the pre-eminent automobile of its genre at the time. Again, Giugiaro would be denied. Below: As with the EB112, the EB218 featured the Atlantic-style rib down the centerline of the body.

Moncalieri, the EB18/3 Chiron. Unlike the EB118 and 218, the EB18/3 was a mid-engined, all-wheel-drive coupe powered by the same Volkswagen-designed W18 engine. It was, in some respects, a follow-up of the EB110. Where the previous two prototypes had been perhaps a little conservative in their style, the 18/3 was not. It was an aggressive-looking coupe which, when viewed from either the side or from a three-quarter rear position, looks a little bulky, because as Giugiaro said, "The W18 engine is quite large and it was not easy to disguise its size in what was a comparatively small mid-engined high-performance coupe."

The frontal appearance was dominated by the modern interpretation of the Bugatti horseshoe grille, which was originated by Giugiaro, this time with the fine vertical bars blacked out and the edges highlighted in chrome. Either side of it were the three-unit headlights, while below was an almost full-body-width, rectangular-shaped air intake. Again the shape of the side glass harked back to Bugattis of the classic era. The rear window was a single piece that exposed the glorious details of the W18 engine. A vestigial Atlantic fin was depicted running along the spine of the 18/3. At the rear were long lighting units running up each fender, and the exhaust pipes poked out from the rear diffuser.

The interior, naturally, was trimmed in the best of materials as would be expected of a Bugatti.

Photographs make it hard to judge the physical size of the 18/3. It sits on a wheelbase of 2650 mm and is 4420 mm long, 1994 mm wide and a mere 1150 mm high, wheel tracks were 1657 mm front and 1648 mm rear while it was shod with huge 265/30 front and 335/30 Michelin tires on 20-inch alloy rims.

Throughout this program, Italdesign people were constantly liaising with key people from Volkswagen. Unveiled at the 1999 Frankfurt IAA, the Bugatti EB18/3 was given a name: Chiron, in honor of one of Bugatti's most famous racing drivers from the prewar era, Frenchman Louis Chiron. Interestingly, VW chose to also display the EB218 at the same auto show.

In parallel with Giugiaro's work, Warkuss's team in the company's Centre of Excellence Design department had also been interpreting the spirit of Bugatti. After considerable discussion and evaluation of what was offered, the Board opted for his design, the EB16/4 Veyron, that has only recently entered production. The mid-engined configuration was believed to be the purest solution for a super-sportscar and it was felt that Warkuss's design reflected both the deep respect felt for the brand and the founder.

This was unfortunate for Giugiaro and Italdesign. Not one of their three Bugatti concept cars was selected for production even though, as Giugiaro was quick to point out, "We satisfied all of Piëch's requirements, but the Board at Volkswagen decided to go with their own design. Even though Piëch and I had a close personal relationship, he was very ethical and professional with regard to that friendship and did not want to be seen to be using it to influence a commercial decision." **AQ**

The third piece of the Giugiaro-Piëch jigsaw puzzle, the EB18/3 was more in line with what Piëch was thinking. The EB18/3, like the Veyron that eventually went into production, was a true mid-engined, high-performance supercar and possibly a modern interpretation of what a Bugatti should be.

SINGULAR ART

The Life and Designs of Art Ross

Overcoming adversity calls for creativity and stead-fastness, particularly when roadblocks occur on both personal and professional levels, and even more so for a young Jewish man living in the first half of the 20th century. To rise to executive-level success in that period's automotive world, such an individual needed street smarts and cunning, a feat lived out by an extraordinary man who impressed designs and touched many lives in the American automotive industry for more than two decades. This is the story of Art Ross, a designer who defied definition.

BY TRACY POWELL

rt Ross was born Arthur Rosenman in New York City, the sixth of seven children in the household of Shekel and Miriam Rosenman. Art was the first in his family to be born in the United States, the others born in the Rosenman homeland of Naroditche, Ukraine. Shekel had fled Eastern Europe's anti-Semitic persecution in 1906, arriving in New York that year, and finally was able to bring his family in 1913. Within the year, Art was born.

For many Jewish families, fleeing persecution in Europe at the turn of the century meant coming to America, usually arriving with a suitcase and little money. Survival meant arriving and remaining "huddled masses" in whatever community they called their new home, as anti-Semitism turned out not to be removed by an ocean. Ill feelings were found in the land of opportunity as well. Perhaps this was the main reason that, when Art was 14 years old and just entering high school, the family moved to Chicago for a new beginning. The year was 1927.

The Rosenman family was part of a thriving Jewish community in Chicago. From the early part of the 20th century, Jewish immigrants flocked to Chicago. By 1948, there were 300,000 Jewish residents in Chicago, second only to New York City (2 million) in America in terms of Jewish urban concentration.

Before his freshman year of high school had ended, Ross found what would become his two lifelong passions: his future wife,

Art Ross's talent can be seen in its early stages, from his first painting at age 14 (above) to drawings from before 1935 such as "Sophisticated Pair" (top right) and this traffic stop depicting Alice, his future wife, at age 18 in a Duesenberg and Art as policeman at age 19.

Ross's ability to craft the human form is evidenced in these drawings from before 1935: "Ten Cents a Dance" (left) and "The Smoker" (above). Below is a sketch for a proposed 1934 model.

Alice Smilgoff, and the arts. Growing up in the Chicago art scene was a rich experience for young Ross, though not an easy way to go. For a number of years after high school, he struggled as an artist. He attended the venerable Chicago Institute of Arts while driving his family's laundry truck, sketching and painting in his free time and honing his skills.

Just before marrying Alice, Art shortened his name to Ross. This surname alteration is believed to have occurred to remove immediate bias in his profes-

sional endeavors. During this period, Ross started searching for a job in the Midwest and in Hollywood. Fortune had it that Ross chose automobiles over the movies: he turned down an offer with MGM.

By the time Ross arrived in Detroit, that city's burgeoning Jewish community was attracting its own clusters of families. The year was 1935, and Ross longed to design automobiles, both inside and out. Early that year he set a meeting with Duesenberg executives. To prepare for his job interview, Ross created a portfolio of four fantasy Duesenbergs. For reasons unknown to us now, Ross declined a position offered him. As Carter Ross, one of the Rosses' four children, said, perhaps he saw the writing on the wall.

Meanwhile, some former Duesenberg employees had switched employers, going to work for General Motors. Evidently, Ross was the subject of office cooler conversation at Duesenberg, because these new GM employees suggested Ross to Harley Earl as a designer for Earl's Art and Colour Section. When Ross arrived for his interview without even his Duesenberg portfolio, Earl directed him to a drafting table and instructed him to draw anything that came to mind. Three hours later, Ross began his 24-year design career with GM. Some of the design elements sketched during his three-hour crash audition were, in fact, used on the 1937 Buick.

From 1935 until the United States entered World War II, Ross held the title of creative designer in GM's Central Office Styling, working on both Cadillac and Buick models. Most notable of the

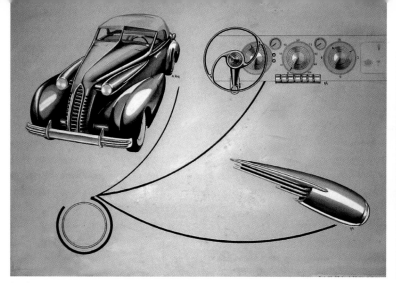

In these sketches of 1934 auto designs we see Ross's ability just before he began his career in the automotive industry. Note the details of the dash in the top left sketch.

models with Ross's influence was the Cadillac Sixty Special, LaSalle, Fleetwood, and the Buick Y-Job show car.

During the war, Ross was assigned to GM's Camouflage and War Services Section, where he illustrated and designed military equipment, includ-

ing the M-1 Hellfire Tank. Ross also designed military instruction manuals, camouflage and small arms.

"Other than Henry Lauve, my father was the only artist at General Motors," said Carter. "There were designers obviously, but no one could do what my

father could do in the world of art, especially of the human figure. Turns out that, during his time in the Camouflage unit, he created a number of soft-porn 'pin-up' drawings and gave them out to servicemen and others at GM. GM execs and VIPs—they loved my dad. He was a very sexual guy. He tied cars, airplanes and women together. It was like one big thing with him."

Near the end of the war in 1945, Ross was rewarded with a promotion to Chief Designer of Cadillac, a temporary spot he filled until the return of Bill Mitchell, who served in the U.S. Navy from 1942 to Dec. 21, 1945. But Ross wasn't embraced by all within the industry, mainly due to the origins of his artistic bent. As C. Edson Armi noted in "The Art of American Car Design", designing cars frequently implies exclusivity, a truism held in high regard among automobile designers, almost to a point of sanctification.

"Men like Raymond Loewy, George Walker, Ned Nickles and Art Ross, who came to design automobiles from a fine-arts background rather than from the custom-car studios, are regularly dismissed by car designers as superficial dilettantes," noted Armi. "Typical are Frank Hershey's comments about Ross, who conceived Cadillac's famous egg-crate 'architectural' grille: 'I think Ross was an artist ... His whole background was different ... Ross, he was

Above: GM's Camouflage and War Services Section, with murals painted by Ross and presumably Henry Lauve. Above right: Work done during WW II. Right: The Ross family at a GM Christmas party in 1948, Art and Alice with (from left) Carter, Nolan and Donnie.

not an automobile lover. Mitchell was an automobile lover. So were all the other people who came from custom-body shops. And that is where you got your designers, because there was no formal education for designers anywhere.'"

Regardless of such opinion, what we are left with are designs among the most beloved from that era. Indeed, Ross is in good company with the likes of Loewy and others who do not hail from a custom-shop background.

"Back in the fifties, some people referred to us as cake decorators," said Bernard "Bernie" Smith, who worked under Ross in the Oldsmobile design studio for four years in the early '50s. "In some regard, that may have been true. Most of the designers at that time did not have an engineering background; they basically came from art schools. That was the case with Art Ross as well. He was a tremendous artist whose talent certainly served him and GM well."

Cadillac's egg-crate grille, to which Armi eluded, was derived from sketches made by Bill Mitchell's Cadillac studio, the earliest of which were Ross's. The overall appearance of the 1941 Cadillacs were made more massive not with over-use of chrome, but with the broad, horizontal-format grille, the first use of the Cadillac hallmark that has stood the test of time.

Ross was also intimately involved in the development of the 1948 Cadillac tail fin. Observing Ross's art and "doodling," it's not far-reaching to imagine Ross handing sketches to Mitchell, who had yet to tone down his own size and scope in styling. Both men were infatuated with aircraft, evidenced in both men's designs and drawings, some of which made it to the production line.

The wide range of artistic medium is another Ross trait, not unlike other fine artists. From pencil, then oils, Ross learned about the latest artist's tool in 1936: the airbrush. Within two years he had mastered its use. In the late 1950s, Ross discovered ink markers and acrylic paints, which he quickly adopted in his own designs and fine art.

POSTWAR PRESENCE

In 1946, Ross was reassigned to Oldsmobile as chief designer. From this post, he influenced some of the most memorable designs for the next 13 years, helping lead the American postwar automotive design effort that made Oldsmobile and GM a world leader in styling and innovation. Bernie Smith wondered if it was more than coincidence that Ross's superior, Oldsmobile General Manager Jack Wolfram, was also Jewish. It's certainly conceivable that an unspoken fraternal bond existed between the two. Whatever the case, Oldsmobile flourished with Wolfram at the helm and Ross heading design.

The winning designs can at least partially be attributed to the air of intense inter-departmental competition. "There was a very fierce competition between Ross in the Olds studio and Ned Nickles in the Buick studio," said Smith. "They were always tossing barbs at one another."

Early on, Ross headed Oldsmobile in pursuit of GM's new Futuramic styling concept, a direction slated to be seen on '49 models. But Oldsmobile was able to beat the other divisions to the punch, as Ross carried over the 1946-48 grille theme with slight modification. The styling was initially restricted to Oldsmobile's Ninety-Eight series, where front fenders were completely blended into the main body; continuation of the fender line became the car's belt line. Not unlike that period's "step down" Hudson and Ed Macauley's modernized Packard, the Futuramic 98 had separate rear fenders that created a muscular back quarter. Thanks to a lower belt line, more glass area was allowed, and a more open interior was incorporated. In the end, Futuramic as

Left: Ross and Bill Mitchell at a GM picnic in 1947. Middle: Ross and Henry Lauve in Indianapolis in 1947. Right: Ross at left shares a story with Rex Mays (second from left) and Mitchell at the Indianapolis Motor Speedway in 1949.

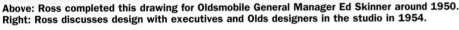

Above: Ross completed this drawing for Oldsmobile General Manager Ed Skinner around 1950.
Right: Ross discusses design with executives and Olds designers in the studio in 1954.

a name was exclusive to Oldsmobile, though other divisions adopted the new styling.

The Olds Eighty-Eight, first available in February 1949, also had Ross's fingerprints all over it. On this model alone were at least three designs patented by Ross: the jet-like hood ornament, the "88" emblem plate, and the combined bumper and grille guard. Despite the model's late arrival in the sales year, the Eighty-Eight quickly became Oldsmobile's best-seller.

Though Ross's excessive use of chrome, and the experimental sense of design in bumper-grille designs, was criticized on early-fifties models, he hit a bulls-eye with the '53 show car Starfire. It first appeared at the GM Motorama in New York City, along with the Buick Wildcat, Cadillac's LeMans and Orleans, and Pontiac's Parisienne. The Starfire was

a futuristic sports convertible with a special 200hp Rocket V8 with 9:1 compression ratio and was fully driveable. Ross brought the Starfire home for Alice to drive. It remained in the Ross garage for more than a year, although Carter remembers that electrical and mechanical problems kept the car off the road for much of that time. The car eventually went back to GM.

Ross scored big on his integration of an oval grille enclosed in the bumper structure, and a sloping hood line that ended with Oldsmobile's "ring around the world" emblem in the center between the headlights. Exterior and interior elements of the Starfire would go on to influence styling of the '56 models.

"I had tremendous respect for him, being one of my early bosses at GM," said Smith. "Art had very strong connections, and he knew where he wanted to

go design-wise. He'd come over and look at my work and tell me I didn't quite have it. He'd sit down on my bench—we worked on benches like piano benches—and tell me to give him my pencil in his slight stutter. He'd take the piece of work I'd been working on for a day and a half and proceed to mark it up, destroying what I thought of at the time as my labor of love. But he was showing me precisely what was wrong and where I should be going with it in the design."

Many times, Ross would sit next to his designers and communicate a dream or vision he'd had the previous night. That would often lead to sketches in a new design direction.

"He definitely was not bashful about giving us direction," said Smith.

Perhaps the most famous model with which Ross was associated is the 1954 Oldsmobile F-88 show car.

By 1954, Oldsmobile was taking its futuristic styling mantra seriously, and went for the sports-car money with the experimental XP-20 project. The fiberglass F-88 two-seater was packed with power: a 250hp 324-cc V8. Coupled with its aerodynamic theme, the car seemed ready to lift off at speed.

"One of the thrills for me in those days was getting to ride in the F-88," said Smith. Smith used to park his car and ride the bus to work to avoid paying for parking. Knowing this, Ross asked Smith if he wanted a ride home in the F-88 one evening. The top was down, and the ride home made for a memorable experience Smith "will never forget." It was an example of Ross's "mellow side," said Smith, "that you sometimes saw, even though he could be a tough guy to work for."

For 14-year-old Carter Ross, ready to go to his grade-school graduation dance, there couldn't have been a sportier, more eye-stopping ride. It was June 1954.

Ross on a rare leisure trip to Florida with host Burt Lyon in 1953.

47

Ross was closely associated with the Oldsmobile F-88. Ross sits behind its wheel above in 1957. Ross stands next to the F-88 in the photo below with Harley Earl in 1954; Earl stands beside another experimental model, the Pontiac Strato-Streak.

"I remember that night vividly," said Carter Ross. "Getting into the car to pick up my date, my dad says, 'Do you want to drive it?' I was stunned. I had only had my learner's permit to drive for a month. As I drove the car over to my date's house, we got a little entourage of cars following this F-88. We reached the house, parked in the front, me in my tuxedo, and my date saw the car. She called in to her parents, and they came out to take a look. Then they started calling in all the neighbors. We couldn't get out of there! But we took off, my dad now behind the steering wheel,

my date on my lap because it's a two-seater."

Once at the grade school, the F-88 again attracted a crowd. Couple by couple, Art Ross drove the kids and their dates around the block. The school principle, teachers and even custodians weren't left out—they too were treated to a ride in the F-88.

"There were probably more people driven in this F-88 than any of the other concept cars," quipped Carter. "When I go back to my class reunions, people remember that as a defining moment in their lives."

The XP-20 project was eventually snuffed, largely

thanks to lackluster sales performance of its close cousin, the '53 Corvette. (Top-producing Chevrolet, with much more clout, also ensured F-88's demise as the Corvette lived on as a division darling.) Two examples of the car were planned, and the one Smith and Carter Ross rode in was later destroyed by an engine fire. The other remained unassembled, and worked its way from E.L. Cord's ownership to Gordon Apker to the current owners associated with the Gateway Automotive Museum in Colorado.

F-88 sold for a house record $3.24 million at the January 2005 Barrett-Jackson auction. "While most of its brethren were destroyed after their debuts at GM's Motorama shows, the gold-toned Olds survived this fate to become one of the most significant vehicles of its era," Barrett-Jackson president and CEO Craig Jackson said at the time.

Both the F-88 and another project, the Cutlass, provided styling ideas for Oldsmobile that would endure for years. Both cars introduced the oval air intake that served as the division's identification, and the trailing edge of the wheel wells opened in a sweep-cut that changed the cutout line from a half-moon to a wing-like opening. Both cars also featured spinner-type wheel covers with turbine-patterned rims, the ancestor of spinner hubcaps now so popular with the younger set.

In 1955, Ross restyled Olds models with a full-oval grille framed at the bottom with a slightly protruding bumper that effectively balanced the exterior styling elements. The new "face" developed into an immediately recognizable Oldsmobile feature. On '57 models, the front-end full-oval design reached its climax, the oval recess wrapping around to the full length of the bumper. "Oldsmobile" was spelled out on the grillework in the recess, and a highly stylized emblem sat above it.

"As we worked on the '58 models, Harley Earl was starting to get down on Ross," said Smith. "Earl

In 1954: Ross with Jack Wolfram (left); with Ed Metzger (above left); at the GM Motorama; and with Bill Mitchell at the Stork Club during the Motorama (right).

would come into the studio once or twice a week. On one of those visits, he commented on the plan view that the lines on the hood didn't look quite right. Art, being much shorter than Harley Earl, wasn't seeing the same thing that Earl was. So Art comes up with this idea to send instructions down to the wood shop to make a pair of six-inch wooden pieces to attach to his shoe bottoms."

The idea was to rise to the height of the much taller Earl in order to see what Earl was seeing.

"Harley Earl walked in on him one day," said Smith. "Art was walking around with those on, and Earl said, 'What in the world are you doing, Art?' Art explained he wanted the same view; Earl got a good chuckle out of that."

Ross's talents were noticed throughout the industry. Over the years, Ross was invited to be a guest speaker on several occasions at universities and arts schools, including Pratt Institute in New York and the Art Center College of Design in Los Angeles.

END OF AN ERA

After leaving his mark on the 1959, 1960 and '61 Oldsmobiles, Ross left GM in 1958 to form his own industrial design firm, Arthur Ross Associates. According to Carter, it was becoming clearer and clearer that Art's freedom of expression was trumped by engineering and economic priorities, as dictated by The General. It was also rumored that Bill Mitchell shared Frank Hershey's sentiments mentioned earlier. Ross left GM with a non-compete agreement in exchange for a five-year bonus payout. At the time, Ross knew that Studebaker wanted to introduce a new sports car, which was soon introduced as the Avanti.

"He really thought about going after the Avanti," said Carter. "But he had two big problems. He didn't know if he could overcome Raymond Loewy's relationship with Studebaker; he thought that was pretty

Ross at Olds Styling in 1956 (left) and acting the part at the Western-themed GM picnic in 1955 (above). Below is a drawing of Alice.

well cemented. Also, he was afraid of GM coming after him as a competitor and losing his bonus. So he backed off. When the Avanti came out, he was grinding his teeth. He said, 'Boy, I wish I could have had that one.' To do a car on your own … he really wanted it, but he honored his non-compete clause with GM."

Heading his own design firm allowed him to pursue new directions in contemporary product design. Over the next 12 years, Arthur Ross Associates provided designs for a diverse group of industrial clients, such as Parker (pens); Tappan and Norge (appliances); Allegheny Ludlum Steel and US Steel (auto products); MacGregor (golf equipment); Shakespeare (fishing and golf equipment); Masco Screw Products (Delta faucet); and, of course, GM, among other companies.

"His illustrations were so good that they sold the design, not the other way around," said Carter. "He also had a sense of what a manufacturer could and could not do, which came from his work at GM. He really knew how to design a product that was acceptable to the owners."

As much as being his own boss was a breath of fresh air in the creative sense, the move away from GM was a blessing for the Ross family.

"I sort of lost my dad in 1946," said Carter. "After the war, he became an executive and he started to disappear. There were mornings when he would come in, take a shower, and leave. He would leave early in the morning; he would come in after we were asleep. And his temper changed; he became very temperamental. He would work 36 hours straight. There was a cot in the studio where you could take naps, and a shower. I didn't get him back until after he left GM. It's true for my dad and for others: General Motors was first in his life. They were dedicated, and they loved GM and their job. These were all men that were driven. It was a very tough place to work."

Art Ross was also known for his love of the ladies, a fact often hidden but not completely unknown to Carter.

"Art Ross was quite a character," said Smith. "He was quite a ladies' man. In the studio, he would take phone calls from ladies, go into his office and we wouldn't see him for half an hour."

Ross's life was cut short in ironic fashion. The mind that dreamt and drew on such high and forthcoming levels was attacked by Creutzfeldt-Jacob Disease

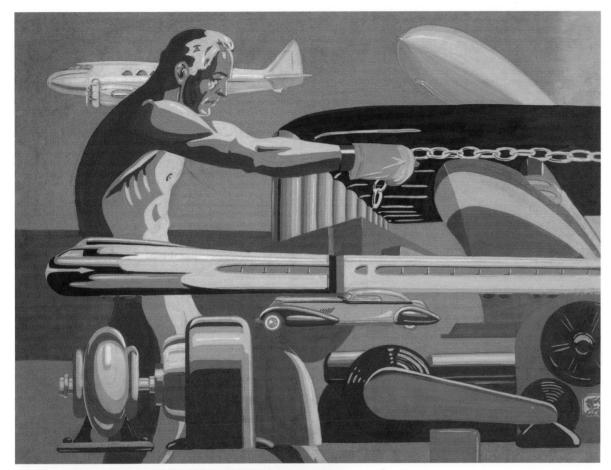

Ross's mural created for GM's Century of Progress (left) depicts man and machine working in concert. His artwork of a Buick racecar completed in 1938 (above) was recently used as the cover art for an exhibition at the Petersen Museum. An example of design from Art Ross Associates (below): a "ski sled" that is conspicuous as a precursor to the modern-day jet ski.

(CJD), the human variant of "mad cow disease," an incurable disease that destroys the brain and eventually kills the person. Art Ross died in Chicago in 1981, at the age of 67, after battling the illness for almost 10 years. (Ross's son Nolan, an accomplished illustrator for the *Detroit Free Press*, also died of CJD in 1997.)

Carter Ross is now on a mission to preserve, and in some cases restore, his father's art, much of which was damaged when the family home flooded. Showcasing Art Ross's talent is near and dear to Carter as he just recently began arrangements with various galleries to exhibit paintings and prints. The art spans from 1928, an oil painting completed by Ross when he was just 14, to 1968, an acrylic abstract of his daughter Monica.

Ross's art was featured, along with other notable works including that of Syd Mead, Joe Oros, Ron Hill and Chuck Jordan, in an exhibition titled "Driving Through Future's Past" at the Petersen Automotive Museum in June 2005. Ross's "Century 60" Buick racecar, depicted in 1938 complete with pop-up headlights and a large rear fin, was the cover art for the event.

Seeing Ross's work on display, in its depth and breadth that crosses industrial and social boundaries, one realizes that Art Ross was much more than an automotive designer. Or an industrial designer, or illustrator. Or even a fine artist. He was all of these, combined. His talent, for all to see, is as atypical now as it was during his lifetime. **AQ**

SWAN

SONG

Last of the Big Packards

T he 1955 Packards were designed to revive an automotive institution, incorporating a new power-plant and innovative engineering inside a body mixing modern and classic styling themes. The Packards were launched in the midst of a long business restructuring scheduled to end by 1957. Less than two years was needed to complete the plan.

BY BROOKS T. BRIERLEY

The passing of automobile body-building pioneer Walter O. Briggs in January 1952 led the series of events that eventually destroyed the Packard Motor Car Company. Briggs Manufacturing Company was the largest independent automobile body builder, making nearly all Packard production bodies since 1941. After Briggs' death, most of the company was sold to its major customer, Chrysler, which agreed to continue building bodies for Packard until other arrangements could be made. Packard decided to revive its once-formidable body-building capabilities by leasing one of the Briggs buildings in Detroit. There was a further setback in 1954 when Packard's series-custom body supplier, Henney, shut down. That quickly took their elegant limousines out of the Packard catalog; a special market was lost to Packard forever.

Coincidentally, Packard was modernizing its motor manufacturing processes, moving away from its vintage East Grand Boulevard complex in Detroit, and consolidating engine, transmission and axle work in its modern Utica, Mich., plant, north of the Detroit. Even so, Grand Boulevard was still produc-

ing chassis, which were shipped to Conner Avenue for completion. The inefficiencies in this three-point procedure combined with the new model to foster a number of quality control issues during 1955.

As the 1955 model year began, nearly two decades had passed since Packard yielded to Cadillac the title of America's most popular luxury car. Even so, the Packard name continued to offer a special magic to both owners and admirers. When General Motors executive Charles "Engine Charlie" Wilson joined the Eisenhower Administration as Secretary of Defense, Cadillac cars made news by quickly becoming the standard for all cabinet heads, except one. The new Secretary of State, John Foster Dulles, insisted on having a Packard. On the other side of the country, movie star Carmen Miranda commanded attention driving around Hollywood in a custom-bodied coupe with a Packard chassis called the Fitzpatrick.

James J. Nance, an aggressive General Electric executive, was appointed Packard's new chief operating officer in 1952. He wanted to refocus the cars more upmarket, muting the emphasis on the mid-

price cars begun during the Depression. The need to reorganize the company, together with the controversial merger with Studebaker, constantly challenged his plans.

By 1955, as Packard began to show signs of turning the corner, it revealed its traditional strength of innovation. This was seen in both production processes and technical features. The special design parts for the new Caribbean convertible were made from low-cost plastic tooling, reportedly the first production use in the industry. Adopting torsion-bar suspension (using a steel bar to function as a spring) was obscure but proven engineering that received rave press reviews. A Hudson engineer, Bill Allison, took a leave of absence to come to Packard to develop it. The technique became known as Torsion-Level Ride. Making sure the new V8 engine had the highest horsepower rating gave the 1955 cars special status. Interestingly, the 1955 Packards appeared to be completely new cars, but included a clever redesign of the 1951-54 bodies by the styling department's Dick Teague.

Along with new V8 powerplants, the 1955 Packard models showed off a clever redesign of the 1951-54 bodies by the styling department's Dick Teague. Left: 1955 Packard Cllipper Constellation, which had a list price of $3,076. Right: 1955 Packard Four Hundred hardtop.

One of the first of the last "big Packards": the Packard Four Hundred of 1955, a darling of design aficionados.

hp for the Patrician and Four Hundred; and 275 hp for the top-of-the-line two-door convertible model named Caribbean.

An interesting attribute of the engines was their being over square, with a 4-inch bore and a 3½-inch stroke (and an 8.5:1 compression ratio). By comparison, the Clipper V8 had a 3 13/16-inch bore and 3½-inch stroke with an 8:1 compression ratio. As the cars made their way through automobile show

PROJECT "A"

Packard popularized the straight-eight engine in the 1920s and stayed with the concept after World War II, as the trend to automatic transmissions underlined the need to develop a more modern V8 engine. The Wall Street Journal reported that the effort to develop these cars was known as "Project A."

The official public introduction of the new V8s was Jan. 4, 1955. The Packard name was now placed only on the most expensive cars to differentiate them from the Clipper, which was "built by Packard craftsmen." Even so, the differences in wheelbase and length of each (127 and 218 inches, and 122 and 215 inches for Packard and Clipper respectively) were so slight as to suggest that Clipper was inadvertently positioned to take away from Packard sales. Each offered two versions of the V8: 225 hp for the Deluxe and Super Clipper models, 245 hp for the Custom Clipper; 260

introductions around the country, they drew a variety of comments. None was better than the headline, "Super-Powered Packard Seizes Spotlight," written about the Caribbean convertible during the Chicago Automobile Show, the week of Jan. 9-16.

Accompanying the V8 engine was a new Ultramatic transmission, Packard's proprietary automatic transmission. The plan was to sell the Ultramatic to other independent automobile manufacturers, as it did some of its engines, to defray development and production costs. At the same time, Packard purchased parts from others such as Hudson. It was called "Product reciprocity" at the time. In 1955, American Motors was reported to be have contracted for the largest of these sales—85,000 V8 Clipper engines.

Among the preparations for the 1955 models was a study of color preferences in dealers' orders. Body colors for luxury cars began to change after World War II, reverting to the bright variety—both single and two-tone colors—seen in the mid-1920s. Packard's survey concluded that color preferences were regional and that women made the majority of color decisions for the family car. Then, Packard organized panels of women in five cities to categorize their color preferences: Washington, D.C.; St. Louis; Oklahoma City; Jacksonville; and Dallas. (It is not clear why major markets such to the New York metropolitan area and southern California were not included.) The panels allowed the company to project future color demands. Colors were labeled Hot (such as red and yellow), Cool (blue, green, pastel), Stark (black and white) and Fashion (trendy hues such as metallic shades). Hots were the choice of 44

percent of the Washington panel but received only 6 percent in Dallas and 0 percent in Jacksonville. Cools were most popular in Jacksonville (65 percent) and Oklahoma City (54 percent), with Washington (32 percent) the lowest figure. The highest rating for Starks was St. Louis with 24 percent, with Washington next at 12 percent. Fashion colors were most popular in Dallas (37 percent) and Jacksonville (35 percent), but least (12 percent) in Washington.

AN INTERESTING NEW DEALER

As the 1955 models were about to be introduced, a new dealership was established in Arlington, Va., Dubois Packard at 3237 Wilson Boulevard. Harry Dubois had been at O'Brien and Rohall, the former Packard dealer in town. One of the Packard's 1955 sales issues was that demand for the Caribbean convertible, the most expensive model, exceeded the supply. The factory would not change the production schedule from 500 cars. James Nance

was reported to have suggested Four Hundred coupes be offered with some Caribbean details such as the twin rear radio antennas. DuBois took the concept much further by adding full Caribbean trim to both coupe and sedan body styles. Those cars were given the dealer's own model name of Esquire. The effect could be very interesting. About 20 cars are believed to have trimmed as Esquires; several survive.

Florida Packard enthusiast Dan Hall grew up in northern Virginia, and visited the DuBois showroom. One of his neighbors bought an Esquire coupe. It was black with a yellow stripe. Hall still remembers his first ride in that car, which included some unpaved roads to test the torsion bar suspension: "The car sailed along like a ship in calm sea." He remembers that, in addition to the Caribbean body trim details, that particular car was also equipped with wire wheels.

DuBois had a number of 1956 models unsold towards the end of the year. That December there was a big sale—just as Earl Anthony was doing in California—to clear the showroom floor. Ten cars, described as "new and company official cars," were discounted by one-third off the list price. Three Esquires were among them; a hardtop with a $6,246 list price was reduced to $4,267.

GREAT BRITAIN

Another interesting example activity during this period was seen at Packard's longtime British distributor, Leonard Williams & Co., located just outside London in Middlesex. Postwar economics led Williams to widen his range of cars to include the Volkswagen, in effect subsidizing Packard, as regular imports of American cars had been restricted until 1954. At London's Earls' Court automobile show in October 1955, three 1955 cars—a Caribbean, a Patrician sedan and a Clipper Custom four-door sedan—were put on display. The models were in a very good section of the show; Bentley was next door and coachbuilder Mulliner was across the aisle.

British road tests of Packards are interesting period pieces today. In general, they mirrored the accolades given by American testers such as Tom McCahill of Mechanics Illustrated, leavened a bit by different driving tastes. In the June 24, 1955 issue of Autosport magazine, sports-car tester John Bolster reported his experience driving a Clipper. This was a special event, the first test by the International Sports Car Authority of an American production car. Bolster went to Leonard Williams to pick up the car and was provided a Clipper Custom sedan. It was

Inset: Some 1956 Packard ads reflected the elegance of the prewar Classic Era. "Ask the man who owns the new one," was the tradition-charged theme. Above: Super Clippers on the transport. Right: Publicity photo tauting the Caribbean's "reversible" front and back seat cushions.

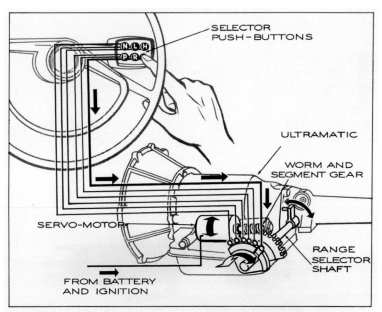

Left: Though Cadillac had become the transportation of choice for the Eisenhower Administration's cabinet heads, Vice President Richard Nixon chose a 1954 Packard Caribbean for this trip. Above: Explanation of touch-button Ultramatic operation.

anglicized a bit with a single shade of dark-blue paint with blackwall tires, but was equipped with left-hand drive. To illustrate the story, the car was photographed on a quay next to the Thames, a quiet, picturesque scene on the outskirts of London. While most of Bolster's story was about the workings of the Torsion-Level Ride, he reserved some of his best compliments for the car's performance, including tips on how to make it accelerate better than a sports car ("really savage acceleration," he pointed out, came from using the "dart" position on the Ultramatic lever). Bolster's conclusion: "You and I, who drive sports cars, are in danger of being passed by a Packard, which is a pretty sobering thought!"

A more conventional appraisal of the Clipper was seen in June 1956 when The Autocar added a right-hand-drive export Clipper Custom sedan to its road tests. Like the previous year's Autosport test, this Clipper was painted a single hue but made a bit more glamorous with whitewall tires. The Autocar was also complimentary: "An unusually comfortable big car, with suspension system of special merit ... Here is something unusual ... astonishingly high speeds could be maintained with complete stability." The Clipper had "a formidable reserve of power that will take it into three-figure speeds without apparent effort." The Autocar took the car to 110 mph and was about to go faster when the driver became concerned about brake fade. Ironically, June 1956 was the month Packard shut down its Detroit production; The Autocar test became instant history.

The importance of the British reviews, which seemed a bit more enthusiastic than their American counterparts, was not so much their effect on a relatively small domestic market but that they disseminated information from a center of commerce. Packard still maintained a worldwide presence and welcomed the publicity. It was no coincidence that Australia was one of the largest export markets for the V8s, many of which survive there today. That was emphasized for the 1956 model year, when a right-hand-drive Clipper was offered. Interestingly, it could only be ordered without power steering.

The year 1955 proved to be only a fair one for Packard. Although American sales registrations rose to about 52,000 cars, from 38,000 the previous year, that was substantially less than the 71,000-plus of 1953 and only slightly better than half of the record 98,000 cars in 1949. That these relatively modest results took place during the automobile industry's best sales year since 1929 revealed a painful loss of market share. Results for new partner Studebaker were worse—1955 sales registrations were virtually flat with 1954 results—and translated into Studebaker-Packard's combined 1955 operating loss of $29 million. That deficit would soon change the business direction of both entities.

A TELLING YEAR: 1956

The 1956 Packards were announced in October 1955, with an early November introduction. Body lines were essentially the same as 1955, with changed body trim offering the most obvious visual distinction from the previous year. Later in the model year, a third line of cars was added sharing the Clipper 122-inch wheelbase chassis and body with Patrician/Four Hundred hood and front called the Executive. That increase in the number of more expensive models was meant to raise the proportion of higher-priced Packards sold, something not borne out in production figures. The proportion of senior cars, including Executive, to Clipper models produced was about 30 percent for both 1955 and 1956.

The similarity of Packard and Clipper body shells and chassis continued to be matched by small differences in finish. For example, the underside of the hood on all models was insulated with a "thick" fiberglass pad. In the larger Packard cars, this pad was faced with a vinyl envelope. Both models were primed for painting with red oxide before being sprayed with four coats of lacquer (each coat separately dried and sprayed). The process was said to include some hand finishing.

These details allowed a well-optioned Clipper to provide the luxury of a car such as a Chrysler New Yorker or Buick Roadmaster. It was really middle-price in name only. Decorator Dorothy Draper and Ed Cunningham of Packard's styling department saw to that. The interior of a Clipper Custom coupe, for example, had a ceiling lined with perforated fabric relieved with thin ribs of chrome, a great-looking design touch once seen on prewar coachbuilt automobiles. Seats with golden-threaded fabric and leather contrasted with a rich-looking gold dash and door panels. Combined with that minuscule three or so-inch difference in length from the senior models, this was by any measure a real Packard.

The apogee of the 1956 cars centered on a new hardtop Caribbean model and increased horsepower. The most robust V8 was tweaked to 374 cid producing 310 hp (5 hp more than Cadillac but rumored 10 hp less than the new Continental Mark II) by a slight increase in bore from 4 to 4 1/8-inches, using elliptical firing chambers allowed a 10:1 compression ratio. There was reported to be a "flat spot" in the previous four-barrel carburetor which was corrected by changing the venturis. Spark plug shapes were longer, too.

Other refinements included an improved torsion bar suspension. The Ultramatic automatic transmission electronic push-button control was now encased in aluminum and given the nickname "driver's piano." Seat backs and cushions were reversible on both Caribbean models, the leather surface meant for day use and brocade for evening. A New York Times story on the new cars indicated a prewar luxury marque option was also available: the senior models could be ordered in any color or color combination (something not verified by that year's Packard salesman's data book).

The press preview of the 1956 cars was impressive. Three were driven by test drivers at the Proving Grounds track: a Four Hundred hardtop, a Clipper and a Caribbean. The press sat in a Clipper sedan parked at the track gate as all three cars whizzed by, each going slightly faster than the car ahead of it. The Four Hundred was first at 100 mph; the Clipper was a bit faster. Then, the Caribbean drove by at 115 mph. Once those cars passed, the gate was opened and the press car entered the track, allowing the press to ride in a car with that same performance.

1956 Packard Patrician.

It's New... America's finest medium-priced car...
and it brings you **Torsion-Level Ride**

Drive the new 1956 *Clipper*
Built by Packard Craftsmen

James Nance also moved to revive Packard's once-rich trove of series-custom models. The most significant revival appears to have been by Howard "Dutch" Darrin, the famous Depression-era coachbuilder who had earlier developed several models for the company. In 1955 he created a European-looking, four-passenger coupe with lines suggesting the wonderful shapes of his prewar convertible victorias, including a slanted classic-shape radiator shell. A small model was built but the project went no further. Another Classic Era coachbuilder, Derham Body Company of Rosemont, Penn., completed a more modest project: modifying a 1956 Patrician with a padded top and small rear window for James Nance. It was not put into production.

The 1956 automotive year was dominated by a business recession in the United States. Overall automobile sales dropped markedly. Studebaker-Packard reportedly defied this turn for the first four months of the model year, doing slightly better than the same period of 1955, but continued operating losses had a traumatic effect on the struggling company's finances. By April, the banks would not refinance their loans. That stopped retooling for the 1957 cars. It was reported at the time that Studebaker-Packard had not drawn down its bank lines of credit for an operating reserve. A long-term insurance company loan had provided most of the company's working capital, which was completely devoured by the large 1955 operating loss. That ruined access to further long-term debt. The amount of money needed was so great as to foretell it could not be raised. Tooling for the 1957 Packard and Studebaker models would cost $50,000,000 to $100,000,000 (accounts vary), with another $8,000,000 or so for dealer subsidies.

The publicity and lack of resolution of these problems destroyed Packard's sales momentum. Draconian measures were implemented to try to stay in business. Packard production ended in June, three months earlier in the model year than expected. Questions were immediately raised about that marque continuing in business.

SOME SALES ISSUES

Comparing individual state-by-state sales registrations of Packard and its competitors during the period of 1953 to 1956 reveals the trend away from Packard, and to Cadillac, Lincoln and Chrysler (and their Imperial and Continental relations). Packard's dependence on both mid- and high-priced sales created a demand that more resembled the multi-range of Chrysler than Cadillac or Lincoln. There is also drama in these numbers: the firm's legendary California distributor Earl Anthony proved the importance of good marketing; he was more effective selling Packard's 1955 redesign than his counterparts in other states. It is not clear why Illinois and Missouri sales in 1955 were virtually unchanged from 1954.

The apogee of James Nance's revival was demonstrated in photographs taken in February 1956. They were 1957 prototypes, all striking-looking cars: a senior hardtop coupe, a Clipper four-door hardtop sedan and a Clipper hardtop coupe. They were said

	California				Missouri				New York			
	1953	1954	1955	1956	1953	1954	1955	1956	1953	1954	1955	1956
Cadillac	11602	13353	17486	16431	2214	2390	2716	2968	9950	11005	15741	14121
Chrysler	10644	6684	11740	10013	3310	1937	2636	1694	19751	13871	18687	13955
Imperial			1639	1535			183	145			1264	1167
Lincoln	4352	4348	4745	5757	884	709	647	726	3279	3530	3534	4231
Continental			91	366			6	34			47	125
Packard	5042	2447	4449	2236	1670	843	842	714	7603	4028	5869	2877

	Florida				Michigan				Illinois			
	1953	1954	1955	1956	1953	1954	1955	1956	1953	1954	1955	1956
Cadillac	2605	3043	4931	5511	8329	9766	11315	9628	7983	9014	11010	10368
Chrysler	2934	2287	3254	2513	8976	5386	8808	4706	11693	7896	10165	7657
Imperial			493	494			670	608			884	764
Lincoln	1140	1206	1224	1837	3067	2470	2385	2844	3033	2705	2445	3372
Continental			36	97			74	68			37	106
Packard	1653	888	1219	667	4858	2361	3417	1320	5301	3413	3579	2134

SOURCE: R. L Polk & Co. as published in *Automotive News*. Note: Imperial sales were not reported separately for 1953 and 1954; the Continental was introduced in late 1955.

Packard's planning. Yet, Packard's 1955 redesign schedule matched Chrysler's. The notable style of the 1957 designs confirm that Packard benefited from the reverse direction of intelligence in the artistic sense, given that these cars have a flawless appreciation of the coming trend toward fins, as well as the strategic, as they matched Chrysler's aggressive two-year redesign schedule.

As Studebaker-Packard's reorganization was announced in the summer of 1956, the existence of these new Packard models was reported as unable to be produced until the spring of 1957. There are also reports that James Nance approached Lincoln in March 1956 to substitute Lincoln bodies for the 1957 model year, as a way of avoiding tooling costs of the in-house models. By one account, the quid pro quo was to have Studebaker and Packard dealers launch the new Edsel. The effort went awry, and may have prompted Lincoln's reported suggestion to Packard's best dealers to change franchises.

Near the end of the summer, a plan was announced to refinance Studebaker-Packard through military contracts to Curtiss-Wright. Certain factories, including Packard's Utica plant, were leased on a long-term basis to Curtiss-Wright to be used for the new contracts. In addition, other Studebaker-Packard assets, including the Packard Proving Grounds, were sold to Curtiss. That provided enough money

to continue. Part of this process included moving Packard production to the main Studebaker plant in South Bend. This move was in name only; the 1957 models were not big luxury cars; in their place were modified Studebakers. That led James Nance to resign. He was replaced by his vice president, Harold Churchill. Packard buyers and longtime dealers such as California distributor Earl Anthony, abandoned the marque. Packard sales collapsed, and in less than two years, production ceased altogether.

Fortunately, much physical evidence of Packard remains. Many of the East Grand Boulevard structures, including the elegant administration building, survive, as do notable dealer buildings such as Earl Anthony's splendid San Francisco showcase on Van Ness Avenue. The Utica factory is now owned by Visteon; nearby, 14 acres of the original 560-acre Proving Grounds site, including the elegant lodge, garages and a short section of the track, are being restored by the Packard Motor Car Foundation to include museums and banquet facilities. A telephone call is all that is needed to arrange a visit to drive a Packard there. About 2,000 V8s are believed to be available to accept the invitation.

The 1955 Patrician V8 (right) at the Packard Proving Grounds test track during its 25,000-mile run. Above: Cutting off the Plexiglas "pheasant windscreen." The gent offering his pocket knife is test driver Carl Altz, at 45 years of age. Altz had helped build the Proving Grounds track in 1927 and stayed at Packard, becoming a company test driver in 1934.

to be designed to share the bodies with Studebaker. There was also some irony in them. During the public discussions of Chrysler's purchase of Briggs in 1953, Packard announced the importance of not allowing Chrysler to build its bodies for fear that Chrysler, a competitor, would have advance knowledge of

The run included a number of interesting details. The "pheasant windscreen" was one of them. Early in the run, a pheasant came up over the guard rail and was hit by a test car. On a subsequent lap, another pheasant jumped the rail and went through the windshield. Something was needed to protect the car. A piece of Plexiglas was sent out from the Detroit airport and taped to the space where the wind-

1957 cars, called "Black Bess," had begun tests at the Proving Grounds in the spring of 1956. In mid-June, as the shutdown of Packard became inevitable, chief body engineer Fred MacArthur took his son Donald, who had just graduated from dental school, to Utica for a ride in the car. The Proving Grounds were technically still open then, but without a full complement of people; some dynamometer testing was still going on. That day, the main gate was locked and had to be opened by a key, which MacArthur carried. "Black Bess" was parked in the repair garage, away from the lodge parking (the lodge had been converted into offices with the lodge's overnight accommodation moved above the repair garages).

As a test mule, "Black Bess" concealed the drama in the forthcoming styling. Its four-door sedan body lines were deliberately misleading, and could be said to resemble an Edsel more than the planned Packard. Only one door had a handle, the others were held together by bailing wire. Underneath the hood was more horsepower for the V8 engine; the Ultramatic transmission was smoother and more durable. Bill Allison, the Hudson employee who had developed the torsion bar suspension for Packard, further tweaked and improved it for 1957. That day, MacArthur took the car over 100 mph, a speed easily allowed by the 31-degree curves in the track. When their drive was finished, the elder MacArthur told his son to take a close look at "Bess." He wanted to be sure the car would be remembered, knowing he would never see it again. The following week, "Bess" would go back to the main Grand Boulevard plant. There it was cut up by big band saws. ◣◰

Above: Servicing the test car at the track gas pump during the run. The stopwatch in hand (left) suggests the holder is one of the AAA men certifying the October 1954 V8 Durability Run. This image includes a good look at the track's straightaway and one of the banked turns. Right: At the beginning of the 20th century, it was common euphemism to refer to having a drink as having a smile. That approach appears to have been revived at the makeshift bar set up to celebrate the end of the run.

TWO RUNS AT THE PACKARD PROVING GROUNDS

Packard's Utica, Mich., Proving Grounds continued in operation during Packard's last two years in Detroit. A 1920s-era complex of Tudor-styled lodge and garages with more-modern outbuildings and a splendid two-and-a-half mile oval track, it had the character of the East Grand Boulevard factory, a direct link to Packard's storied past.

The last great technical feat at the Proving Grounds was the 25,000-mile Durability Run officially introducing the V8 engine in October 1954. A Patrician four-door sedan was given the honors to perform this continuous night-and-day run for 238 hours, 41 minutes and 44.3 seconds. The average speed was 104.7 mph including pit stops. The run was conducted under AAA auspices.

shield had been. The Plexiglas would scratch if the windshield wipers were used, so the wipers were turned off, something not really needed when driving over 100 mph.

The end of the run called for a celebration, with a makeshift bar setup. A very good selection of beer was included.

Not two years later, an impromptu run at the track signaled Packard's end. A well-disguised mule of the

Tale of Two
Packed With Packards

Despite the demise of the Packard Motor Car Company 50 years ago, auto enthusiasts have had the good fortune that the company produced such well-made vehicles that owners, for the most part, chose to care for them. Most every auto museum today has at least one Packard on the floor, but in the state of Ohio, there is not one, but two museums solely dedicated to the marque.

BY RICHARD S. MANDEL

Museums

It should be of little surprise that one of the Ohio museums is in the town of Warren, which lies midway between Cleveland and Pittsburgh. The community is where Warren Packard found success, through business interests in hotels, a hardware store, a lumber mill and an iron rolling mill. The town of Warren is also where his sons William Doud Packard and James Ward Packard founded Packard Electric in 1890, and it's that company's success that led to Warren being the first community ever to have all-electric street lighting. It was, in part, an arduous three-day, 54-mile return trip to Warren from the Winton factory in Cleveland that provoked J.W. Packard, already exploring development of a "motor wagon," to create with his brother what eventually would become the Packard Motor Car Company. And to Warren is where J.W. returned, after his term as President of the company for the first six years following its move to Detroit.

Remnants of the Packard family's heritage and contributions to the town can still be found in Warren. While the family mansion no longer exists, there are other houses and buildings that had been owned, at some time, by the family. And there is Packard Park, overlooking the Mahoning River on land donated by the family in 1911. In 1955, the WD Packard Music Hall, constructed with funds from a family trust, opened at the southern end of the park.

For many years, a large public swimming pool existed on Packard Park's north side. After the pool was taken out of service, the City of Warren offered the property as a permanent site for Packard memorabilia. The pool was filled in, and the adjacent equipment and activity building was torn halfway down, then reconstructed to house what officially opened as the National Packard Museum on July 4, 1999, the first day of a Packard Centennial Celebration in Warren.

The museum focuses, in equal portions, on local history through the lens of the Packard family, Packard Electric Company and Packard Motor Car Company. There are a wealth of displays containing family and business documents, personal knick-knacks, and photos and art showing the Packard businesses that were in the region. There are displays of products from Packard Electric, from the company's earliest days of light bulb manufacture, to more recent ignition wire products and electronic assemblies, the latter under the Delphi Electric name. Mementos abound, such as commemorative items that were distributed to employees, advertisements, showroom banners, and even some tooling items found in a long-forgotten back corner vault of the original

The front entrance to the National Packard Museum in Warren, Ohio, is a creative take on a gigantic Packard front end.

trucks in 1917. Pneumatic truck tires evolved quickly after that first 1917 run, becoming so reliable in such a short time that in 1918, seven Express trucks carrying Boy Scouts completed a 3,000-mile excursion along the East Coast without a single blowout.

The museum also proudly displays a 1903 Packard Model F runabout. Terry Martin, a local resident, auto restorer and Packard enthusiast for most all of his adult life, restored the car as a copy of "Old Pacific," the vehicle that completed the second tour from San Francisco to New York by an automobile (although the Packard had far fewer breakdowns than the Winton that preceded it). In 1983, Martin, along with Tom Fetch, grandnephew of Old Pacific's original driver, retraced the journey driving the restored Model F, now nicknamed "Old Pacific II." Modern highways certainly improved the time it took to drive

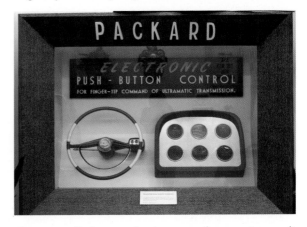

Above: One of the earliest models, a 1903 Model F runabout, found at the museum in Warren. Right: An informative display of Packard's ingenious Ultramatic transmission.

Warren automobile factory. The museum also hosts tours of sites that bore the Packard name in the area.

For those who come to see rolling stock, the museum's small size limits the display at any given time to less than 24 vehicles, with others rotated through. Additional space is on its way, however, as the museum was awarded funds in August 2005 for an expansion.

All decades from 1900 on are represented, and there is a Packard motor from a WWII PT boat on display. Of particular note is a 1941 Model 1908 Custom Super 8 One Eighty Touring limo with a LeBaron body; this was the last vehicle purchased and owned by Elizabeth G. Packard, the widow of

J.W. Packard. There is also a 1916 Twin Six Touring car that was owned by Henry B. Joy, Jr., son of Packard Motor Car president Henry Joy Sr.

In another corner, a 1917 Model E three-ton Packard truck stands apparently ready to serve again as a Goodyear Wingfoot Express, one of several vehicles that were part of a plan to establish the first interstate trucking route by making regular nonstop runs from Goodyear's Akron tire factory to the company's tire-fabric mill in Connecticut and back, a 1,540-mile round trip. The Goodyear-designed body was set up to accommodate a two-man crew, with the first sleeper cab in the trucking industry. The truck also had pneumatic tires, novel since hard, solid rubber tires were standard equipment for short-haul

the one-cylinder runabout across the country, as it reached New York in 23 days rather than the 61 days of the 1903 run. Terry, who is also a member of the board for the National Packard Museum and has authored articles and a book about the early years of Packard, recalls being passed by "bikers on Harleys, who would give hearty thumbs up to the plucky duo rolling along at 25 mph in their tiny open Packard."

Martin, it should be noted, is well known for his extensive knowledge of the Packard family and the pre-Detroit days of the automobile company bearing their name. The first four chapters of "Packard: A

History of the Motor Car and the Company," a book that was published in 1978 and distributed by Automobile Quarterly, were penned by Martin, detailing the Packard lineage back to their arrival in America in 1638, and continuing to October 1903, when the company's production lines began operation far from Warren. Terry still drops by the museum, and if you should chance to meet with him, be prepared for some very engaging stories that make the exhibits in the Warren museum come to life.

Above: Also at the National Packard Museum in Warren is this 1917 Model E three-ton truck used as a Goodyear Wingfoot Express, one of the first such trucks commissioned in an attempt to establish the first interstate trucking route.

AMERICA'S PACKARD MUSEUM

Just a few hours drive to the Southwest of Warren is Dayton, home to the world-famous United States Air Force Museum at Wright-Patterson Air Force Base. To Packard enthusiasts, however, the real treat is just south of downtown Dayton.

Robert Signom, a Dayton attorney who also owns a small collection of Packards, had purchased a boarded-up building after months of negotiation, intending only to use the space as a place to keep his cars. After the purchase was made, a friend, on tour of Signom's new acquisition, commented, "This is a really neat building. Where is the Packard museum, anyway?" It was a "Eureka" moment — Signom chose to establish what is often referred to as America's Packard Museum, officially opening the doors in 1992 under the name of the original dealership — The Citizens Motorcar Company. The building and its history is special, as it first began business in 1917 as a dealership in an area of Dayton that also saw dealerships for Auburn-Cord, Pierce Arrow, and the less spectacular Fords, Chevrolets and others. The Citizens dealership chain was the third oldest purveyor of Packard automobiles in the United States, and the Dayton building sold and serviced Packards until WWII. After the war, the building was occupied by other automobile companies, and then used as a regional warehouse for an automotive parts company.

The service department's original floor lifts, made by Joyce, were found still intact in the service area, along with the mechanics' suspended hose reels. Original wood doors that separated the main sales floor from the used-car department were found upstairs in the building, and were subsequently restored to their place. Service people from Joyce came in and restored the floor lifts, and the 12,000-lb-capacity elevator that moved vehicles between the building's floors was found to require only moderate servicing and updating. The original linen drawings for the dealership later turned up at a local garage sale, revealing a design in the style of noted architect

Albert Kahn, who was first to successfully apply poured concrete to building construction, and was later selected to design and create Packard's buildings on East Grand Boulevard in Detroit.

Architecture is not all that is shared with the Packard offices. Hanging on one wall of the restored dealership's main showroom is a six-foot-diameter copper plaque bas-relief of a 1908 Model S, which once adorned the Packard conference room in Detroit. Behind glass on another wall is the original Certificate of Incorporation of the Packard Motor Car Company. There are personal business letters and other items on display, as well.

Cars from Signom's collection, beginning with a 1928 526 coupe-roadster identical to one once owned by his father, share the floor of the main sales salon and the used-car floor along with many donated and loaned vehicles. The collection then extends to another adjoining building that had been added behind the main dealership in 1936. It is equally striking to note how many vehicles are on display in superlative, unrestored condition, as it is to see so many that are described as "this is one of two that exists," and "this is the only one of its kind." The collection has three Darrin-bodied Packards, for example, including a 1940 Super 8; a 1940 180 with a sedanca top that was first owned by popular character actor Donald Meeks; and a 1941 180 with side mounts and running boards that had been made for the New York Auto Show, from where it was immediately purchased by John "Shipwreck" Kelly, former New York Giants football player and owner of the Brooklyn Dodgers NFL team, for his wife, socialite Brenda Frazier.

Other cars from well-heeled owners include a 1933 Super Eight touring car that belonged to the William Procter family (of Procter and Gamble), and a 1946 Custom Super Clipper that was first owned by the Dupont family. Both cars show only a few spots of wear where the paint has been buffed and polished down to the undercoat — otherwise, they are in the same livery as the day they were delivered. One interesting detail to observe about the Procter car is that the family wanted to not be overly ostentatious when driving about, so the car was ordered with all normally chromed surfaces, such as the headlights and bumpers, painted black.

The collection has one of the two 1942 180

Founder and curator Robert Signom in front of the Citizens Motorcar Company in Dayton, also known as America's Packard Museum. On right is the Citizens' main showroom, complete with a 1930 Model 734 Boattail Special.

Above: This one-off 1928 "Jesse Vincent Speedster" was once driven by Charles Lindbergh, a gift of Carl and Narcelle Schneider.
Right: This 1941 Darrin-bodied 180 was made for the New York Auto Show, where it was immediately purchased by "Shipwreck" Kelly.

Clippers that has survived to this day, and the only 1943 Packard convertible known to exist. Recently added to the collection is a 1930 734 boattail speedster, one of 11 to survive, although major restoration of this particular car was necessary — the vehicle had been found in Argentina with the bodywork cut and removed from behind the cab, then replaced with a pickup bed. The 734 now gleams in showroom-new glory again, complete down to its Pilot Ray driving light. One of Al Capone's last cars, a 1946 Custom Clipper, is here — clean, unrestored, and with no unusual holes in the bodywork. And there is a supercharged 1957 Packard Hawk convertible, the only one of its kind because its owner, Studebaker's last chief engineer, had the hardtop removed to show his corporate chiefs the potential of the design. One can only wonder, looking today at the top-down P-Hawk, if anyone had noticed just how handsome and sporty the car was, as compared to the Thunderbirds and Corvettes at that time.

One of the most unique vehicles in the museum does not, in a sense, actually exist. In 1998, fellow Packard collector Carl Schneider came to Signom and showed him a recently acquired 1951-dated set of construction blueprints of a Packard, as rendered by Italy's Pininfarina studio. Packard management, at the time, had turned down production of the custom design. Schneider offered the blueprint for display in the museum, but Signom suggested, "Why not just build the car?" The resulting fastback bears the familiar 1951 Packard front and rear bodywork, Pininfarina tags, appropriate interior, and a straight-eight Packard engine coupled to a period five-speed gearbox. When the car was shown at an East Coast show, several Bentley owners noted that the design resembled a Pininfarina Bentley that had been manufactured in the early fifties, which Signom

Top: Unrestored 1933 Super Eight touring, originally purchased from Citizens by William Proctor, gift of Robert and Sonia Turnquist.
Bottom: A 1942 180 Clipper on loan from Steve Maconi.

suggests may have stemmed from the Pininfarina Packard design exercise.

In an alcove off the used-car sales floor, the museum has reproduced a small parts department, with various parts on shelves and in the glass display case. A local carburetor repair shop, when it closed several years ago, yielded a Carter promotional display that sits atop the display case. Nearby lie several styles of trunks, including one designed to fit in place of a running-board spare tire.

Across from the parts shelves is another glass display holding aftermarket speed components. On top is an Edmunds intake manifold made for a Packard straight-eight, mounted to a display board and fitted with dual single-barrel carburetors. In the case is a complete Iskendarian cam kit in its original packaging.

Speed was not all that alien to Packard, and two fine examples reside in the American Packard Museum. First is the original 1904 Model K known as the Grey Wolf, which captured the world land speed record of 1904, then went on to place fourth in the inaugural Vanderbilt Cup race that same year. Across the floor rests a 1928 Speedster personally commissioned and owned by Colonel Jesse Vincent, the brilliant chief engineer of Packard. He asked his staff for a lightweight 126-inch frame from a six-cylinder model, and an aluminum roadster body with no fenders, lights or other items that would add weight, then added the largest eight-cylinder engine Packard manufactured at the time. Legend has it that Vincent used to tear through Detroit streets in the car, regardless of day or night. And it seemed that Vincent was somewhat small in stature, as suggested by a hidden footpeg that could extend from one side to ease getting into and out of the cockpit. The speedster returned to service in September 2004, when it was entered in a 500-mile San Francisco-to-Santa Barbara race that passed several times through the mountains adjoining Highway 1. Signom, who drove the car along with friend Kelly Gibbs as navigator, says the car won handily and ran fine the entire distance, although they found three days spent

1952 Packard Pininfarina fastback. On loan from Carl and Narcelle Schneider.

structed along one wall inside of the rear building, using wood-and-glass panels that once served as divider walls in a Packard dealership in Cleveland to create the front wall of the room. (That former dealership, by the way, is now part of the Cleveland Clinic Hospital Complex, although on one side a visitor can still see most of the words, "Packard Motor Car Company," chiseled into the marble façade.) The museum brought in a desk that may have come from the president's office. The library officially opened, dedicated to Robert and Sonia Turnquist, in February 2005.

The museum maintains an on-site restoration shop for museum vehicles, divided between the basement and the second floor. There's a paint booth that can

above the roar of an un-mufflered straight-eight to be a bit taxing on their hearing.

Besides automobiles, the Dayton museum has another of the marine engines used in WWII, this one of a non-magnetic design for use in a mine-sweeper. There are also commercial marine engines that were used to propel pleasure boats like those built by Chris-Craft.

Aviation history is also present at the Citizens Motor Car Company. One stand displays an early Liberty engine, while another stand shows a DR 980 nine-cylinder rotary diesel engine that Packard built between 1929 and 1931. The design was immensely

practical, as it had no ignition to create electrical interference in those early days of aircraft radio. It was a combination of the Depression and the death in a crash of Lionel Woolson, project manager and chief test pilot, which ended production.

A Rolls Merlin engine is also on display, as a reminder of the WWII Rolls-Royce co-production contract made with Packard. And there is a Packard J-47 jet engine, built under license with GE, which was used in the B47 bomber, later to evolve into the B52.

In 1965, "The Packard Story: the Car and the Company," was published. About 35 years later, that book's author, Robert Turnquist, along with his wife Sonia, established the Turnquist Packard Library by contributing a large personal collection of Packard-related literature to the museum. A library was con-

handle large assemblies, and the building's original ducting system, for removal of vehicle exhaust from the service area to the outside, was found to be sufficiently intact to be brought back into service. All of the museum's collection is maintained to operable condition, including a small fleet of Packard limousines available for rental by the public for weddings and other special occasions. The museum has served as a meeting site for The Packard Club (PAC), an international organization of Packard collectors and enthusiasts. Additionally, the museum is an avid supporter of The Packard Motor Car Foundation, which Signom helped found in 1997 as a non-profit chari-

Above: The 1952 Packard Pininfarina fastback.
Right: Citizens original 20-foot porcelain and neon sign.

table foundation, dedicated to the preservation of the products, history and properties of The Packard Motor Car Company. The foundation's first project, which is nearing culmination, is the restoration of the remaining acres of the original Packard Proving Grounds in Utica, Mich. Purchased from the Ford Motor Land Development Company, the property still contains the architecturally important, Albert Kahn-designed lodge buildings, plus garages, a timing tower, the Lindbergh hangar, an elevated water storage tank, a portion of the test track, and the Grand Entrance gates.

Part of the space beyond the second-floor paint booth is taken up by shelves and tables covered in parts. These are not from cars being serviced, but rather have been donated to the museum for use in restoration, or for sale to other collectors, in turn helping fund the continuation of America's Packard

Museum. One can find semi-orderly containers of knobs, various radios, trim, even ring-and-pinion gear sets still wrapped in paper and boxed in Packard packaging. On first glance, one senses what Howard Carter must have felt on his first glimpse into the tomb of Tutankhamun. It might even be said that seeing the breadth of so many Packard parts in one place is almost as stunning as touring a museum entirely dedicated to a single American auto manufacturer that ended business nearly a half-century ago, whose elegant cars wait to be loosed on the streets once again. **AQ**

Arthur Stone (above) and his Packard collection, housed in the Fort Lauderdale Antique Car Museum.

MR. STONE BUILDS HIS DREAM MUSEUM

It is a museum that was inevitable. Arthur and Shirley Stone began collecting automotive memorabilia, with a primary focus on Packards, back in the mid-1940s. His business, Buning the Florist, Inc., was already doing well and on its way to becoming a chain of thriving florist shops across several southeastern states. When Arthur retired at the end of the last century, he had not only amassed enough vehicles and bric-a-brac to start a museum, he had also the makings for one.

"I had the land, and I had a warehouse," says Stone. "I had come across photos of a Packard showroom that was in Florida in 1922, and I thought, 'Yeah, I want to build that.' I had salvaged trusses and wood in the early '50s from an old factory building that was being torn down. Those trusses were 50 feet wide and 12 feet tall, and made from Dade Count pine. I put them in my warehouse behind a stack of concrete block, so nobody would find them. They're holding up the roof of my museum."

With such a knack for collecting and saving materials, Stone ensured the Fort Lauderdale Antique Car Museum would be packed with treasures. The 22 Packard automobiles displayed in the 18,000-square-foot space are all pre-WWII vehicles, starting with a 1909 Model 18 speedster. Other elegant notables would include a 1916 Model 1-35 Twin-Six Town Car limousine with C.P. Kimball coachwork; a 1920 Holbrook-bodied Model 3-35 limousine; and a 1929 Model 645 dual-cowl phaeton with body by Dietrich. There are a few utility vehicles here, too, including a 1915 Model E 2½-ton truck that had been owned and maintained by the St. Lawrence Starch Co., which was eventually bought by General Mills. Stone purchased all of the cars in the collection, often in 80- to 100-point condition.

But the museum presents much more than cars. Much, much more. There are several hundred horns and sirens, glass bud vases, clocks and hood ornaments. A visitor will find groupings of spark plugs, carburetors and vehicle lights. Aftermarket gear-shift knobs. Exhaust whistles. Greasers and oilers. Motometers. Not just one or two, but hundreds of each category. And there is still more, which led to decorating one corner of the museum to resemble a vintage Texaco service station, complete with gravity pumps, oil-dispensing cans, signs and a sloping roof that was unique to Texaco.

At 86, Arthur Stone still climbs into one of his cars and takes it out for a spin. He's delighted to share his collection with the locals, as well as the world, and the museum's guest book indicates that the world has been in attendance. The cars are in a trust now, and the city of Ft. Lauderdale has given a grant to add an additional 7,000 square feet to the structure. Will that be enough to display the entire collection? "Never!" declares Stone, who knows that tomorrow may well bring another interesting addition to the museum.

American Motoring Through the 1940s

The decade of the '40s and a couple of its Hollywood personalities. Opposite: Ronald Reagan and Jane Wyman during their acting days, alongside a 1949 Lincoln Cosmopolitan. Above: Rita Hayworth showing the spirit that brought the Homefront through the war.

It was a time in which the recently labeled "America's greatest generation" came of age, during a period when the country's men and women proved their true grit in the face of world war. It was the 1940s, a decade that defined the awesome might of America's military resolve in the waking of "a sleeping giant," thanks to an automotive industry that moved swiftly to transform its factories and distribution channels to meet the massive wartime demands. Evolving technology and a growing fascination with aviation combined with a later period of prosperity to create a decade that marked a distinct dividing point in automotive design and production.

BY MICHAEL L. BROMLEY

On the evening of May 8, 1945, a switch was thrown, and for the first time in four years the Washington night sky was split by the white Capitol dome and its piercing "Freedom" statue. Victory in Europe was official. Up in New York harbor at eight o'clock that same evening "the lady with the lamp" lit her torch, then she herself was drenched in a 26,000-watt blaze from mercury vapor lamps newly installed for the occasion. With the fall of Germany, the War Production Board declared an end to the Atlantic coast "brownout" it had ordered during the 1942 U-boat scare. The electric news bulletin of the Times Tower in New York City, and the colored lights of Broadway theaters, restaurants, and hotels meant that America would soon go back to being America again.

Yet all summer war raged in Asia, and Americans braced for the inevitable and thousand-fold more bloody fighting that would surely follow an invasion of Japan. America was desperate for normalcy, and through 1946 the wish for normalcy outran the truth. The Jan. 1, 1947 cover of Automotive and

Germany and Imperial Japan. The "Arsenal of Democracy" and the "American industrial might" were synonyms for that greatest industry in the world. Steel, rails, ships, construction and all the other great trades alone couldn't sustain the diverse parts and machining businesses that built the automobile, and upon which the war conversion so depended. Certainly, victory took far more than Willow Run, but for that massive diffusion of motoring over and across America there was no such immense industrial scale, distribution, expertise and

Above: The night of Dec. 7, 1941, Washingtonians gathered before the White House at the news from Hawaii. A few days later, a deserted Pennsylvania Avenue and a darkened White House spoke the fearful reality of America going to war. Right: Pearl Harbor gave new force to scrap drives and new value to junk heaps, such as this pile in Butte, Montana, and this wrecked car, now "Bound for Japan."

Aviation Industries said it for all in wishing for a new year: "With Full Production, No Strikes, Abundance of Materials, Lower Prices." Happy thoughts at the end of 1946, which the magazine labeled "a Year of Calamity."

Before it all began, the American automobile set destiny for Nazi

infrastructure that America put to war. Converting toy factories and bottling plants to armaments was all good, but those simpler industries couldn't design and build tanks, airplanes, motors and electronics—and all at the same time. The American automobile industry was capably diverse for its unique market and market demands. A list of the industry's contributions startles more for the diversity of output than its production numbers: from the 207,400 binoculars to the 12.5 billion rounds of ammunition, or the 245 million artillery shells to the four million-plus engines, 2.6 million trucks and to 27,000 aircraft, the extent of the industry's service was as broad as its depth. And the contribution extended well beyond statistics. From its origins, the industry built and carried along with it such crucial wartime sectors as labor, engineering, science, aircraft, glass, steel, textiles, machining, plastics, rubber, and petroleum, and pushed them all to make it better, faster, less expensive, and more innovative.

Then there was the automobile's step-brother, petroleum. Only that motoring-obsessed people could have built America's world-shattering ability to fuel all-out war. The automobile's thirst and the networks that satisfied it, from extraction and distillation to transport, from the beginning put America in the strongest position of any combatant. A Nazi general admitted it upon surrender to Patton's Third Army: "How can you expect to win a war when you have no gasoline and no horses?" he told interrogators. Energy, of course, was the German problem from before World War I. Japan, too, long suffered it, and saw in its acquisition reason enough for war.

By mid-1941, with severe rationing in belligerent nations, and the Lend-Lease program supporting Britain with American oil, neutral countries such as Brazil, Chile and the United States were forced into energy conservation regimes. The Office of Price Administration (OPA) urged Americans to avoid wasteful driving and to tune engines for better performance. Here came calls for those brief interludes from the First World War with "Motorless Sundays." In early August, the OPA imposed a nighttime curfew on gasoline sales along the East Coast. Despite the curfew and the suggested maximum "fair" prices for gasoline, the politics of isolation yet demanded peacetime policies, even as industry and the country largely prepared for the war that finally came on Dec. 7, 1941. As plans for gasoline rationing in the East began in April 1942, the OPA turned to price fixing across the nation as a counterpart to the enforced scarcity.

For America, was there life without cars? City-bound sportsmen fretted over how to escape to favorite streams and forests. Manhattan golfers rented a bus to take them to rural clubs. Traveling salesmen argued for the same exemptions as doctors.

"The Precious Spare." No car owner was to keep more than five tires, with the rest turned in or sold to the Government, with gasoline ration cards supplied as an incentive. For many Americans, as this cartoon depicts, it was a difficult separation. One man complained that after selling six tires to the government for $8.80, he blew another tire which cost him $13.40 to replace.

Above: Gasoline rationing began on the East Coast in May 1942. Hit by huge losses of ocean tankers to German U-boats, the problem came in distribution, not production. Initial shocks of rationing hit cities such as Washington, D.C., over the summer, as seen here at this Wisconsin Avenue gas station in July. Left: Ration cards became a national commodity, with A, B, C, and X cards allowing holders different amounts and priorities. Pictured here, a gas attendant checks a ration card against the license plate.

Left: The most famous of the automobile industry's wartime efforts was Henry Ford's final, Herculean task of creating the huge Willow Run factory that produced an amazing 8,685 B-24 Liberators. No less important were the diverse and cumulatively huge efforts of the entire industry, as depicted here with anti-aircraft guns built by Chrysler (above) and the Bren Gun Carrier built by Ford (below).

Americans agreed in concept to rationing. Its practice was another matter. Those seven million new cars of '40 and '41 were itching for exercise. They were not easily kept down. Rationing had started that spring with tires and sugar, and soon enough, gasoline in the Eastern states. In May, some 10 million car owners were to register for rationing cards according to need. The coveted "X card" allowed for unlimited supply. Congress, naturally, voted itself X cards. And, naturally, there was a rush on gasoline the days before rationing began. People carried off what they could in cans, barrels and milk bottles. The program was hotly debated through 1942, but it didn't, as they say, hit home, until America's full entry into the war in Africa later that year.

Patriotism and legal consequence sharply cut pleasure driving, which was reflected in empty beach resorts and little weekend traffic. Nevertheless, abuse never ceased. In late 1943 the OPA opened 9,500 cases of rationing violations of all kinds, especially

Above: Fifty-caliber machine guns were produced at a GM sparkplug plant. Right: U.S. Marines and their motors.

in gasoline. Often working with government insiders, "chiselers" sold fake or stolen ration cards. The burden of enforcement was placed upon gas stations, which were held liable for taking fake cards. An investigation into Chicago black markets concluded that 800,000 gallons a day went to "illegitimate channels" in that city alone. "From the investigation so far," said an Illinois official, "one would be led to believe that the gasoline supply of the country is being appropriated first, to meet the needs of military uses, second for the requirements of lend-lease and, third, to keep the black market supplied." The government appealed to citizen patriotism, saying such things that the sum of fake coupons passed by one counterfeit ring could have fueled 1,000 bombers over Berlin for five days.

OPA prices throughout the war were from 16 to 20 cents a gallon, which meant a heavy subsidy for the East Coast that at times cost producers over a million dollars a day. Thus committed to mandating supply and demand, the OPA toyed with pennies and gallons, a tight game of carrot and stick between ration card availability, quantities allotted, and penny-sized price changes. Motorists were not fooled, and complained that increasing rationing cards while cutting allotments amounted to more, not less, restriction. The best reply by the OPA was that the situation merely required "voluntary cooperation by motorists who want us to win the war." Patriotism or no, every adjustment busted against prices and demand, with black markets the release valve. Afterwards the Chicago Tribune reflected on the rationing: "There was always plenty of gasoline for anyone willing to pay the black market price." The problem, and it remained so throughout the war, was in delivery and its enforced price, not in production.

Cars, of course, were also rationed. In 1941 there were just shy of 30 million autos registered nationwide. At the war's end the number had dropped by five million. Given the missing 3.5 million annual new cars, relatively few, then, were scrapped during the war as compared to normal replacement cycles. As the nation adjusted to rationing and petroleum production kept pace, rising used-car prices reflected continued auto use and unfilled replacement demand. In late 1943, an $800 '41 model went for over $1,100 in New York, and was worth even more on the West Coast. That July the OPA announced rationing and price limits on used cars. The inevitable black market was even more unmanageable than that of gasoline, for illegal "private deals" between individuals proved impossible to halt.

Above: Tires were among the first commodities rationed during wartime. Most other rationing in automobile use, such as in speed, as seen here with lowered national "Victory Speed" of 35 mph, was intended to save rubber. Right: The government allowed production of specified "war model" or "Victory" bicycles in order to satisfy the need for personal transportation, or to make the appearance thereof, in the face of rationing and automobile shortages. The bicycles sold for around $33 and despite the good intentions, didn't do much to save gasoline or effectively move people about. Americans wanted and needed their cars.

PEACE TIME CHALLENGES

Peace, however, brought the first painful scarcity in automobiles as anxious demand roughed up peacetime conversion. Against OPA controls, used-car prices again jumped following the trickle of new cars that began in late 1945. Tracking

a demand spike in service calls that doubled in June 1945, the AAA warned against impatience. "Any motorist who chases the rainbow of an early delivery of new cars to the neglect of the unit of transportation he is driving may face the necessity of walking before his dreams come true," warned the group. Through 1946, OPA prices for used and new cars were near parity. A prewar Fordor sedan in mid-1946 was listed for $946 as against $1,068 for a new model—assuming either could be found at a

dealer that played by OPA rules. The racket played by "numbers men" was to buy new-car wait-list contracts and resell them for a large premium. A "blonde," it was reported, bragged at a party that she

had made $15,000 by "getting on many lists" and turning cars over within hours at $500 profit each. She didn't realize that she was speaking to a car dealer. "Everybody's in the automobile business these days," the man lamented.

As the OPA released its hold on wages, or merely planned it, strikes hit industry-by-industry. A general strike shut down GM in late 1945, which left only Ford and Hudson making cars at the close of the year. Through the first half of 1946, every major builder experienced closings due to some strike, be it in coal, electricity, copper, steel, railroad, glass, or directly against makers. Worst of all were strikes in parts suppliers. Ongoing price controls worsened wartime material shortages, such as in lead, which sold at OPA prices well below international rates. In September, GM considered shipping cars without batteries. Even if final assembly plants avoided strikes, labor turnover plagued production. "I think it is a restlessness as an aftermath of the war," GM president Wilson wrote in an October 1946 mea culpa—or, more properly, a culpa everyone else—as to why The General was producing cars at half 1941's rate. Whatever production stability could be found in labor agreements was more than offset by the continued price regime. As Wilson explained, "I don't know of any good reason why a Chevrolet should sell for $100 less than a Ford or Plymouth if it was $5 more prewar ... In other words, we got a little extra squeeze." The squeeze also came of the wartime employment bonanza. GM's 222,322 hourly workers made 55,000 vehicles a week in 1941; in 1946 there were 267,731 workers producing 28,000 cars weekly at wages half again higher.

Left: The national shame: Japanese internment. The store-owner's protest couldn't have been better punctuated than with the car parked out front. Above: The U.S. Army Freight Depot, 1943.

Needless to say, the 2.2 million new cars built from 1945 to 1946 barely met normal replacement demand, much less the four war years of stifled demand. Continued material shortages and labor agitation kept 1947's production well below 1929's magical mark. And just in time for fuller recovery, consumer spending collapsed in late 1948 with an unfortunate meeting of renewed wartime credit rules and depleted wartime savings. Reinstalled in the name of Truman's inflation fighting, the "Regulation W" required one-third advance payment on installment sales not to exceed 18 months. Two of three buyers demanded the maximum credit allowance. Business tripped over suddenly piled inventories as consumers stayed home. And factories that could sell cars couldn't produce enough in the face of continued steel shortages and strikes in steel, rails and elsewhere.

Unlike the overly enthused postwar year of 1919, the immensity of World War II and its hold on the economy meant more realistic peacetime expectations from carmakers. Most threatening was labor and the government's relationship to it, and just how much of the New Deal had survived the war. Despite the strikes and despite Walter Reuther's various nationalizing "Reuther Plans," the core rationale of the New Deal evaporated with the Truman Administration's misguided and fearful expectations of a return to mass unemployment. As it turned out, factories fretted over labor turnover and absenteeism as much as over union organizers. Packard president Christopher complained of a woman who didn't show up for work because, she explained, her "spending money was backing up," and she needed more time to get rid of it. With high wages, high employment, and the government caught up in larger problems around the world, the labor-

Democracy was the triumph of World War II. The Everyman's car was no longer a thought. Now, every man and woman would have a car, and it would be distinctively one's own. Well, maybe not everyone could have a Cadillac, like this 1946 Model 62 (left). Building postwar cars was no easy thing. In late 1946, Packard President George Christopher warned that continued price controls ensured scarcity and low production. Costs were skewed by increasingly expensive parts, which bumped total costs against OPA price ceilings. The OPA countered that the industry was greedy. With November mid-term elections approaching, the Truman Administration gave to mounting popular pressure and poor industrial results, and sped orders for "decontrol" of the economy. Automobiles were finally relieved on Nov. 9. Just as importantly, restrictions on civilian rubber use were lifted two weeks later. New cars could now be shipped with spare tires. (Pictured on right is a postwar Packard Clipper.)

industry relationship solidified into mutual distrust and general agreement. Most important for both was the end of wildcat strikes, which had plagued the prewar period of 1941, and for which neither Big Labor, Big Business, nor Big Government held any sympathy. While fiercely opposed by labor, the 1947 Taft-Hartley Act (passed over Truman's veto) reflected as much Labor's consolidation of its 1930s takeover of the automobile industry as the limits the Act imposed on it. Altogether more troubling for car makers than labor were price controls and material shortages, especially in steel, but not only there. In 1946, priority food purchases by a United Nations relief program caused delays in automotive castings operations, as crucial corn meal-derived binders went lacking. One company sent agents into the countryside to buy corn directly from farmers. Where shortages meant delays, any rush to cure it caused more expense. Nash and Ford turned to costly air freight to keep assembly lines open with crucial supplies.

We like to think of possibility as the war's aftermath. But it was Truman's hardened realism the nation followed, not the dreamy vision of Woodrow Wilson, the confident normalcy of Warren Harding, or the blind optimism of FDR. Solutions were no longer found in politics or organization. It was technology that set dreams afloat, and Americans were infected with its possibilities. But the old barriers to entry, to the much-anticipated new Chrysler, having been set after WWI and firmed in the Depression, were, after the Second World War, built impossibly higher. Only a few tried. Only one made it, and only for a time.

When the home-front hero Henry Kaiser and Packard executive Joseph Frazer announced their partnership a month before V-J Day, possibility ruled. Admirable though it was, Kaiser ultimately proved unable to carry the modern load. On so many levels, the Kaiser story tells the larger way out of WWII. Postwar deprivations, price controls, and labor costs, agitation and turnover assured near-

impossible difficulties. Kaiser, however, brought a clever postwar solution to auto making by converting Willow Run from bombers to automobiles, and at government-subsidized rent (and, later, with federal loans). Sharing the huge plant with Graham-Paige, it was to be a model for peacetime conversion. And right away it fell to postwar reality. The Graham-Paige second coming succumbed to a union cat-fight between AFL and CIO branches of the UAW from different Graham plants that argued over who would represent the workers at the consolidated location. Between union bickering and wildcat strikes, Graham decided to shut down and hand things over to a new start as part of Kaiser-Frazer, new union contracts and all. Graham workers replied with a 16-1/2 mile protest around the gargantuan plant, the better part of which had to be covered by roaming automobile pickets.

Truly, for Tucker, for Kaiser-Frazer, for Hudson and for Nash, or for any builder, the late 1940s were tough. While anyone who built a car from 1946-1950 could sell it, getting cars out was trouble top to bottom. Kaiser managed through the 1946 shortages, through delivery problems from the Continental engine plant, through steel shortages and labor trouble, to build its 100,000th car in September 1947; it was disastrously short of Henry Kaiser's January brag of sitting on orders for over a million Kaiser and Graham cars. The real test came in 1948, a year that tore into the industry and foretold its later form in the Big Three-and-a-Half. One can easily lament the fall of Kaiser. The company weathered the '48 recession, but only just, and then just in time for post-recession labor strife and, in the summer of 1950, the arrival of the Korean War and its return to price and credit controls, steel shortages and tax increases. While wartime work

brought military contracts and full employment, it killed the return to 1920s promise. Instead, 1930s same-old prevailed. Kaiser couldn't withstand the crush of larger competitors' synergies, and soon, too, along with the Nash and Hudson and the Packard and Studebaker combinations, consolidation with Willys. Out of the Korean War, GM, Ford and Chrysler hit full production, and the independents were buried in a price war that only mass production could afford.

In the end, things automotive ended where the war started, with the automotive order little changed from before. While no longer demanding "industrial democracy" and the like, such as nationalizing excess automobile capacity and steel production, Reuther's UAW commanded the field.

Above: The name of a true postwar corporate innovation came up during the Tucker trial, when Tucker's attorney tried to deflect the government's arguments against itself with the biting comment, "Kaiser-Frazer didn't get indicted and they got $44 million from the government, didn't they?" Indeed, part of how Kaiser-Frazer got as far as it did (and admirably so) in postwar America was with federal subsidies in the Willow Run lease, military contracts, and RFC loans. While Kaiser didn't commit stock fraud, the company did have some trouble over its stock issues and corporate reporting. Below: A memorable postwar design, the 1948 Ford F-1 pickup.

To build a car, you worked with the union. While the independents proved incapable of launching either the low-priced miracle or the next Chevrolet or Chrysler, they did move styling and tested consumers and markets, including the ever-elusive American small car. Though theirs marked a small percentage of the market, the presence of the independents gave dealers and consumers important alternatives, and their production numbers added up to a whole bunch of cars, however buried beneath the totals of the giants. Above all else, the independents gave to the nation as much as any when the need arose in 1941, and again in 1950.

What did resonate new after the Second World War was an invigorated automotive democracy, and

one far beyond that almost socialistic sameness of the Model T that so appealed to 1930s reformers, and that by then had been thoroughly rejected by the buying public. Across market categories, consumers looked to cars to find and express themselves. Gone forever was the hyper class distinction of town cars, replaced by styling and automotive choice at all price points. The value shift brought the high and the low ever closer. The Classic Era was gone, having given in to the people's rule which, after all, was the great American triumph of World War Two. ▲Q

GOLD STANDARD

Stanley Gold's Porsche Passion

While jogging on a California beach in 1990, Stanley Gold was 10 minutes from a life-changing event: While leaving the beach, he passed a driveway where a Porsche 356 was parked, a mundane 1964 coupe that had a "For Sale" sign on it. Something about the shape of the car caused Gold to stop. Gold owned a new Porsche 911 at the time, but he was fascinated by the 356. Perhaps it was in his blood.

BY PHIL BERG

ecalls Gold, "I had a 1970 914," back when his family was much smaller. "The kids got bigger so we had to sell it. So then we had Mercedes station wagons. When I finally got back to sports cars, the kids were off to college, and in 1989 I bought a Porsche Carrera. I was interested enough I actually read all the manuals and signed up for the Porsche club. And I quickly learned that the people having the most fun were the 356 guys. I thought, 'By gosh it would be fun to see if I could redo an old car.'"

So Gold bought the 356 he saw near the beach and commenced a year-and-a-half restoration of the little blue car. He wanted to enter it in concours events, but soon learned his competition included more unique models, and special low-volume Porsches.

"I had it all redone, and I was into taking it to concours events," he explains. "But soon I found out that while it was a nice 356 there were more desirable cars. There were Speedsters and Carreras, and so for about 10 years I entered all kinds of cars in concours events. In 1998 a guy in the club told me, 'You've got to go racing.'" Gold had never raced before, so he started driving in tours and rallies. Eventually that led to several vintage racecars and a steady schedule of racing in tracks around the West Coast.

"I raced a 2.0-liter '69 911 on a regular basis at Fontana, Thunderhill, Las Vegas, Phoenix, Buttonwillow and Willow Springs," he says, finally entering a car in the Petit Le Mans event in France. "And in December 2002 we were at 150 mph down the Mulsanne straight in a 1964 904 and cars were going by me and I was going by them, and it was the best thing I could ever do."

As the cars began to pile up, Gold's collection became more sophisticated, and now he has more than 15 very unique cars. It's been a long process to build the collection, but it didn't really follow a pattern. "I sell one, I collect one. You buy a car if the spirit moves you, or how much money you have to spend on it, or if you do a deal and you decide to treat yourself to a car. Or if you don't do a deal, and you have to sell a car. I'm not sure I know how I do it."

But the collection is constantly changing and evolving. Some cars that Gold has sold, he misses. In the early 2000s, he had a 904 that he loved, but he also had his sights set on an Abarth model. "I wanted a really good one." He had sold an Abarth previously and then asked the purchaser if he could buy it back. "I kept hounding the guy I traded it to and I said, 'How about selling it back?' and he says, 'How about selling me the 904?'" Gold also bought a 911 Carrera like the one he had when he got back

Porsches are collector Stanley Gold's forte, neatly kept behind sliding doors that open into a brick courtyard.

into the Porsche collecting frenzy. "I'd like to get another Speedster in here someday, and I'd like an RS America kind of car. For a long time I had a 550A Spyder, and I sold that. I had three or four full concours cars, but I couldn't drive them. I didn't have the nerve to drive the 550 Spyder, because it was perfect. I didn't want to get it dirty. I sold it but I'd like to go back and buy another one."

THE STORAGE SOLUTION

The bulging collection presented a huge problem for Gold, who lived in a residential neighborhood and had a small two-car garage behind his house, which was on a small lot. "I had two or three cars in other garages, I kept a couple at a beach house, but the salt air is not great for them. They were always in somebody else's garage."

In 1997, Gold was in his yard, when another car-collecting neighbor came by walking his dog. "I told him I had a new car to show him," recalls Gold. "He came and looked and said it was a beautiful car, but the garage was junk. It was an old pre-war garage. Homeless people used to sleep in it."

Then another house on Gold's street went up for sale. This was on a double-size lot and had a small carriage house in the backyard, with tennis courts

Inside Stanley Gold's garage is an open floor plan with exposed, solid wood beams overhead. The garage can comfortably hold up to 12 cars.

In addition to the spacious garage is a room like "grease pit" (below).

adjacent to the small building. So the Golds moved, with the idea that they would build a much bigger garage and move all the cars into one place. They designed a building that sits where the tennis courts used to be, and its roof is continuous to the carriage house. At the same time they built the garage, they renovated the small house.

Each side of the new garage has driveways, one of which separates the garage from the carriage house. Above that drive is Gold's office, which opens into the second floor loft in the garage. "I like open plans, with wood beams," says Gold. But the architect had added some extra beams the Golds didn't like. "So then everybody from the contractor to my wife changed it," recalls Gold.

The floor is made of Italian ceramic tiles. As the workers were laying the tiles, there was an odd batch that didn't exactly match. Gold's wife asked the workers about the mis-matched tiles and they responded: "This is a garage, lady," recalls Gold. But to the Golds, the structure was much more, and they insisted that the tiles match.

The sliding doors open up to a brick courtyard in the backyard, but there are no doors or windows that open to the alley. "I didn't have any problems meeting building codes," explains Gold. "I did not want any windows to the alley, because I didn't want people busting in, or looking in, so we backed it all up against a solid wall.

"When we have affairs here and other people bring their cars, I'll open the driveway between the garage and the carriage house so we can use both driveways. All the cars park along the grass and park everywhere. It looks really nice with all the lights on at night."

Inside, the space is wide open for cars, with no posts. "We didn't want lifts, because this is a big rumpus room," says Gold. So to allow access for working on the cars, Gold designed a basement room with a grease pit opening to the display floor. "We needed the neighbors to sign off because the pit is a non-conforming use because it's underground. So our neighbors would come by to look at this pit under construction because they had to sign off on it. One guy asked, 'What are you doing, building a bomb shelter?' Another one asked, 'What are you making, a ritual bath tub?' And I said, 'Stop it; this is a pit to change oil.'"

The kitchen lines the alley side of the garage, under the loft lounge and office. Next to it is a wine cellar, a cigar humidor, and a cache of champagne magnums. A staircase in back leads down to the room-size oil-change pit, which is full of cases of oil and tools. "I personally don't do anything," Gold admits. "There's a full toolbox, so you can do any work. I have guys come in and do it."

Gold also had central air conditioning installed in the garage, which can hold up to 12 cars. "For years

Central air conditioning and a loft are inviting touches.

we never had air conditioning in our house down the street," he says. "Finally I put air in the top floors, and when I built the garage, my wife asked, 'What are all those ducts for? You mean the cars get air conditioning and I went for all those years without it?'"

The garage turned out as good as Gold had imagined. "I came out one summer day, they had dug the foundation. I had a glass of wine in my hand, and was sort of overlooking my empire here," Gold remembers, telling his wife that he could fit a dozen cars into the new garage. His wife answered that she could get 75 people for dinner in the new garage, too, if the cars were moved onto the lawn. "She told me, there's a full kitchen in it, there's a bathroom in it. We'll have parties out here."

But for Gold, having a safe home for his Porsches in his backyard is his reward. ◢◣

Villa d'Este

A Decade of
Concours d'Elegance
1995–2005

A rguably the finest show of classic and collectors' cars in Europe has been taking place annually since 1995 in the beautiful parks of Villa d'Este, Villa Olmo and Villa Erba near Como in Italy. This location was chosen not only for its optimal location and scenery but also in remembrance of the original Concours d'Elégance, the coveted gathering of upper-class international society in prewar days.

BY FERDINAND HEDIGER
PHOTOGRAPHY BY MICHEL ZUMBRUNN

A BRIEF LOOK INTO THE HISTORY

The area at the southern end of Lake Como is blessed with an exceptionally mild climate. It was populated in Roman times and was selected by high-ranking clergy and noblemen as a place to build sumptuous mansions and palaces. The foundation walls of Villa d'Este date back to the 14th century. After years of splendor the building fell into decline, changed ownership several times, was restored and extended, and finally purchased by a group of local businessmen in 1873. Soon it became a luxury hotel of splendid reputation, which continued to grow for more than 130 years. Since 1963 the excellence of the hotel Villa d'Este has been assured by the Droulers family.

The Villa Olmo, named after a giant elm tree growing nearby, also has a long and checkered history. It became the property of the township of Come in 1925 and was selected four years later by the Automobile Club of Como for their first Concours d'Elégance for automobiles. Between 1929 and 1949 a total of 10 automotive beauty contests took place in the great parks of Villa Olmo and Villa d'Este. These fashionable shows of the latest models of automobiles and coachwork had originated in France. One of the earliest was staged in 1927 in the Parc des Princes of Paris.

Above: The 1932 Concours d'Elégance of Villa d'Este. Right: Concours cars line up around an old plane-tree in front of Villa d'Este in 1996.

The first Concours d'Elégance in 1929 attracted 55 participants from Italy and abroad presenting the finest and most modern automobiles. The overall winner was Celestino Piva with a truly beautiful Isotta Fraschini Tipo 8A with a Faux Cabriolet body by Cesare Sala, the famous coachbuilders from Milan. Apart from many Fiat, Lancia, Alfa Romeo, Itala and O.M. models, there were American cars from Reo, Cadillac, Stutz, Graham-Paige, Lincoln and others, as well as Talbot, Hispano-Suiza, Voisin from France, a lone Minerva from Belgium and a "Grosser" from Mercedes-Benz participating in the event. For 1930, not less than 93 cars participated, but already the field consisted mostly of Italian makes. Due to the political situation, foreign automobiles were no longer popular and the event became more and more a showcase of domestic

ers. However, it took time to convince the public. It is easy to be smart in hindsight, but still a bit difficult to understand the verdict of the judges, to award the Coppa d'Oro to an unwieldy, swollen cabriolet with covered front and rear wheels by Stabilimenty Farina on a dated Lancia Astura chassis. The wonderful, small Cisitalia 202 coupé by Pininfarina, which would later become an exhibit in the Museum of Modern Arts of New York, was declared a class winner only.

Two years later, most of the cars looked much more up to date. Again some of the milestones in modern body design, such as the 166 Inter coupé by Touring or the Ferrari 166 MM barchetta were not considered for the top awards. The Alfa Romeo 6C2500 Sport

Fabrizio Giugiaro of Italdesign in pleasant company at the 2003 event.

with berlina body by Ghia won the Coppa d'Oro. The Superleggera coupé by Touring on a similar SS-chassis won the first prize of the public referendum, and became known as the famous "Villa d'Este."

The next Concours d'Elégance of Villa d'Este was planned for 1952 but never materialized.

makes and coachbuilders. Despite the inflation in the awards, which peaked in 1931 with 113 entries and a total of 91 prizes, foreign cars in the list became the exception. An occasional Rolls-Royce, Mercedes-Benz, a Hispano-Suiza with a Pininfarina body, some Packards, Cadillacs and Reos, and the famous Duesenberg J re-bodied by Hermann Graber were the only notable foreign minor-award winners in the next years. Almost invariably the first prizes went to Italian makes and coachbuilders.

The first postwar Concours d'Elégance of Villa d'Este took place in September 1947. While Kaiser and Frazer launched the first "full width"-bodied serial production car in America, most European manufacturers developed their postwar designs only reluctantly. The most advanced coachbuilders were faster in picking up the new idea of integrated fend-

RELAUNCHING THE CONCOURS D'ELÉGANCE IN 1986

Announced as the 11th Concours d'Elégance of Villa d'Este in 1986, the basics had changed considerably. Instead of the latest models of automobiles and coachwork, the entries consisted of historic and collectors' cars. They had become increasingly fashionable in Europe and overseas. The contest revived by Franco Lombardi and others took place in June and the winner of the Coppa Villa d'Este was an Isotta Fraschini Tipo 8A SS of 1927 with a torpedo body by Cesare Sala.

Yet it took another nine years to make the Concours d'Elégance of Villa d'Este a regular annual event in April. Two of the initiators of the second re-launch in 1995 were the famous Italian automotive historian and writer, Angelo Tito Anselmi, and Urs Paul Ramseier, president of the Swiss Car Register and closely linked to the history of coachbuilding in Switzerland.

In 1995 the star entry was a marvelous 1931 Isotta Fraschini Tipo 8B with an Imperial Landaulet body by Castagna. It not only won the first award of the jury but also the grand prize of the public referendum, the Coppa d'Oro of Villa d'Este.

One year later the public poll awarded the trophy to a Bentley 3 ½ Liter of 1934 with a fixed-head coupé body by Hooper. The grand prize of the jury went to an Alfa Romeo 8C2900 B of 1938 with an open spider body by Touring Superleggera.

Alfa Romeos were successful again in 1997. A 6C2500 Sport cabriolet of 1942 won the public ref-

Above: Angelo Tito Anselmi (left), one of the initiators of the relaunch in 1995. Right: A 1928 Mercedes-Benz "S" cabriolet by Saoutchik, Paris, at Villa d'Este in 1995. Opposite: 1938 Alfa Romeo 8C2900 spider by Touring, Best of Show 1996.

erendum prize and a 6C2500 SS of 1950 with coupé body was awarded the jury trophy, both coachbuilt by Touring Superleggera. In the following year the event was canceled.

BMW PATRONAGE

By now the Concours d'Elégance of Villa d'Este was well established among the owners of historic and classic cars and there was a big field in 1999. BMW Group took over the patronage of the event. The trophy was awarded to a Rolls-Royce Silver Ghost of 1911. A stark Mercedes-Benz SS sports roadster of 1929 with coachwork by Corsica of England won the BMW Italia trophy.

For 2000, a re-organization was effected. BMW Group clearly defined the goal: Villa d'Este is to remain the best and most coveted Concours d'Elégance of Europe. Some extracts from the introduction in the program booklet written by Karlheinz Kalbfell, at the time marketing director of the BMW

Group and project director for Rolls-Royce, show their thoughts, intentions and dedication: "BMW's innovative approach notwithstanding, and in view of the rich history of the company and its brands, we continue to place enormous importance on cultivating our heritage. This led to the establishment in 1994 of BMW Mobile Tradition with the task of preserving the company's past and coordinating all activities that are related to BWM's history. Our involvement in the Concorso d'Eleganza forms part of this heritage promotion. It is our way of demonstrating our respect for the great automotive past, which will be so gloriously brought alive by many distinguished car marques. The event offers an exclusive and elegant framework for the presentation of

historic cars which convey to us the enduring nature of top-quality products and cultural values."

The organizing committee with Jean-Marc Droulers as chairman and Franco Lombardi as concours coordinator had set up a fine program for the participants and visitors. The jury consisted of nine distinguished experts from all over the world under the leadership of Carlo Felice Bianchi Anderloni, the former president of Touring Superleggera.

Forty-three of the finest historic, classic and sports cars were entered, ranging from the tiny Cisitalia coupé and Lancia Aprilia cabriolet to the majestic Rolls-Royce Phantom III, from an Auburn V12 boat-tail speedster to the Ferrari 166 MM barchetta. The Coppa d'Oro was won by a Bugatti T.57SC Atlantic of 1936 and the jury awarded the BMW trophy for Best of Show to the Alfa Romeo 8C2900 of 1938 with superb Touring spider coachwork.

In 2001, an equally illustrious field was admired. In addition to the contestants of the Concours d'Elégance, there was a small section of racing and

rallye cars, a fine range of historic BMWs, a number of Rolls-Royce cars by members of the Royce-Royce Owners Club and a display honoring the masterpieces of Touring, Milano. The Coppa d'Oro went to an Alfa Romeo 6C2500 SS "Villa d'Este" cabriolet by Touring. The jury trophy was won by the one-of-a-kind 1961 Aston Martin DB4 Jet coupé by Bertone and the black Ferrari 340 America barchetta by Touring of 1951 received the BMW Italia award.

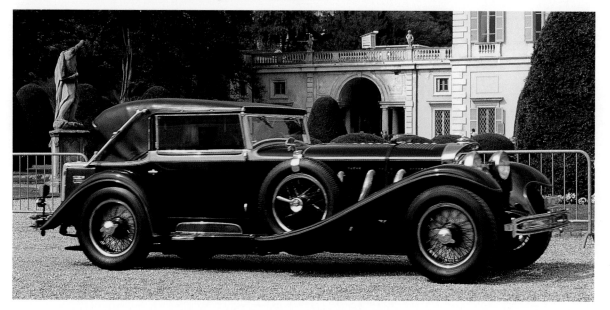

Above: 1948 Isotta Fraschini Tipo 8C cabriolet by Boneschi at the 1997 event. Below: 1930 Mercedes-Benz "SS" cabriolet C by factory coachwork Sindelfingen seen in 1999.

CONCEPT CARS AND PROTOTYPES

In the following year the meeting became even more attractive. Not only were there many famous classic marques and models to be admired in the regular contest itself, but a new category for concept cars and prototypes had been created. Ten entries represented the latest trends and fashions in coachbuilding by famous designers.

BMW displayed four different Mille Miglia coupés and roadsters of prewar days. Some of their concept cars and "art cars" created on various models by modern artists such as Andy Warhol, Roy Lichtenstein and others were shown as well. To celebrate 90 years of Bertone, a great exhibition covering much of the company's activity was staged on Sunday in the park of Villa Erba. The futuristic Alfa Romeo BAT 5 prototype of 1953 with its aerodynamic body was on the lawn. Once again a line of old, luxurious Rolls-Royce cars were present as well. In the 2002 event, the Coppa d'Oro was awarded to an Alfa Romeo 6C1750 SS cabriolet Royale by Castagna of 1931. The jury trophy went to the Ferrari 342 America 1953 cabriolet by Pininfarina and the Design Award was won by the Alfa Romeo Brera prototype, 2002, by Giugiaro, Italdesign.

For the 2003 event, 48 outstanding cars had been selected to participate in the regular Concours d'Elegance and 13 prototypes and concept cars for the Design Award. BMW Group presented the brand-new flagship of their Rolls-Royce division, the impressive Phantom. This year a special display on

their historic models from the museum. The new Rolls-Royce experimental 100EX model was presented. For the 85th anniversary of Zagato, some of their extraordinary models of sports-car design were shown in the park of Villa Erba. From their famous spiders on Alfa Romeo chassis from prewar days to the latest Aston Martin roadster of 2004, the wide range was admired by enthusiasts. The Coppa d'Oro was awarded to the 1933 Lancia Astura with double-phaeton by Castagna. The BMW Group Trophy went to a 1957 Ferrari 250 GT California spider by Pininfarina and the Design Award was won by the Alfa Romeo 8C of 2003.

Contrary to the years before, the 2005 meeting was tarnished by rainy weather. Especially on Sunday, when the public was admitted, most of the open cars and some of the prototypes etc had been covered with plastic sheets. Some cars made only a brief attendance. Of the many cars especially brought to celebrate 75 years of Pininfarina, only a few remained uncovered during the wet event. BMW Group had brought its Isetta and its Type 507, both of which had been launched 50 years previous. The public referendum award, Coppa d'Oro, was won by Jeff Fisher with his 1951 Ferrari 212 Export spider by Vignale. The jury decided the 1964 Alfa Romeo Canguro coupé by Bertone that was brought in from Japan should be Best of Show and win the BMW Group Trophy. The 2004 Peugeot 907 prototype coupé, designed and created by the manufacturer, won the Design Award.

In the past 10 years, the Concours d'Elegance of Villa d'Este has established itself as the finest contest for historic and classic cars, as well as concept cars and prototypes of Europe. The special exhibitions by BMW Group, displays of various famous coachbuilding companies and collectors' clubs make a participation or visit even more desirable. The continued patronage of BMW Group, Mobile Tradition, a worldwide automotive network, an efficient organization, and a competent and un-biased jury of experts will make certain that Villa d'Este will remain a coveted meeting place of fine cars for decades to come. ◢◣

Above: 1948 Talbot-Lago T26 Record cabriolet by factory in front of Villa Olmo in 2000. Right: 1953 Ferrari 342 America cabriolet by Pininfarina, Best of Show by jury in 2002. The proud owner, Art Zafiropoulo, is second from the left, with the American restoration crew.

Sunday gave a good overall view of the 35 years of activities of Giugiaro and Italdesign. Some outstanding examples like the BMW Nasca C2, the Bugatti EB 112, both of 1993, or the Aston Martin 2002 prototype could be compared. A 1955 Maserati A6G berlinetta by Frua, a 1930 Rolls-Royce Phantom II convertible by Binder, Paris, and a 1937 Delahaye 135MS with the flamboyante cabriolet body by Figoni & Falaschi were the trophy winners. The Design Award went to the Pininfarina Rossa spider of 2000.

Lovely weather once again greeted the participants and visitors of the 2004 concours. BMW Group celebrated its 75th anniversary of car production and brought several of

1955 Ferrari 375 MM berlinetta
by Pininfarina.

1964 Alfa Romeo Canguro coupé by Bertone, winner of 2005 Best of Show and the press award.

Connecting Quinby and Brooks-Ostruk

Influencing TWO Automotive Generations

J.M. Quinby & Co., located in Newark, New Jersey, was one of America's oldest coachbuilders. James Quinby began the business in 1834. It quickly became the leading carriage maker in the state (likely helped by Quinby's interest in politics; he served as mayor of Newark from 1851-53). By 1857, about 200 men worked there. In sharp contrast was the Brooks-Ostruk Co., located across the Hudson River on West 66th Street in Manhattan. It was strictly a 20th century firm, incorporated in February 1917, entering the automobile body business without having made carriages. The new firm soon enjoyed a name for innovation and splendor, and became known as one of the most prestigious coachbuilders. Little did each company's founders realize that one day they would forge a unique link.

BY BROOKS T. BRIERLY

Quinby entered the automobile age not only as a body maker but as a chassis manufacturer. Its young thirty-something superintendent and draftsman, Walter Yelton, a Kentucky native who graduated from the carriage maker's Technical School, surely helped provide the perspective to make the transition. Emerson Brooks, an equally young New Jersey businessman, began working at Quinby in the

in the touring events and competitions that promoted everyday use of the automobile.

Then, it was no surprise that, in 1899, Quinby built not only an automotive body but a complete electric automobile. The first cars were made to order that spring—for pleasure driving. Later in the year, there was a plan (called "scheme" at the time) to manufacture 4,500 of these vehicles for delivery

The following year, Quinby returned its entire focus to body building.

Early Quinby customers reflected the wide variety of automobile marques then available, such as bodying the seven French CGV (Charron, Giradot and Voight) assembled in Rome, N.Y., during 1902 and 1903, and the Jennis, made in Flourtown, Pa., from 1903 to 1905. Only two test cars had been built before production was abandoned. Both Jennis models had Quinby five-passenger touring car bodies. One of them survives, providing the highest survival rate of any Quinby-bodied marque. Quinby's first very grand automobile body appears to have been a seven-passenger touring on a 1904 Scott chassis (built in Baltimore) made for Harlan Whipple, the president of the Automobile Club of America.

Above: The Quinby exhibit at the 1905 automobile show included this handsome limousine on a French Decauville chassis. The details in the window shapes seem very advanced for the time. Right: The George N. Pierce Co. included a Quinby limousine body on its 1905 Great Arrow cars.

late 1890s, providing the firm with another progressive voice. The company sent Brooks to Europe in 1902 to learn European design. Brooks' interest in motor cars also led him to participate in the Automobile Club of America (now the American Automobile Association or AAA). In this parallel capacity, he could be seen

and general livery use in a newly formed company headed by James E. Hayes. One of the partners was to be J. Herbert Ballantine, the brewer. To deliver ale and beer (among other things) throughout New Jersey by way of a fleet of silent electric vehicles was a great idea but one that never came to pass.

Quinby joined the automobile body builders early in the 20th century as an innovator, making light-weight aluminum bodies. Aluminum not only was

Above: This very elegant town car on a 1906 Simplex chassis was trimmed with jewel-like side lamps. Note the similarity of passenger compartment lines to the Pierce opera coach. Below: This 1907 Fiat was owned by American diplomat Larz Anderson. A fine example of Quinby's open body styles (note the second curve in the rear fender) was photographed by the Anderson estate carriage house in Brookline, Mass. It is still housed there today, as the building has become the Larz Anderson Auto Museum.

lighter but offered a dramatic savings in the number of coats of paint and varnish needed compared to a wood body—eliminating the filler and guide coats. Quinby worked with the Aluminum Company of America to produce a "Tulip" touring car body in 1902. A variation of this style took a more majestic name in Europe where it was called "King of the Belgians." Quickly, the "King of the Belgians" style became the rage for touring car design here. In 1903, as French manufacturer Panhard was negotiating to license Messrs. Smith & Mabley (later known for creating the Simplex automobile) to assemble their cars in New York City, there was a parallel agreement to have Quinby build the bodies in Newark.

Unfortunately, a number of other foreign firms also contemplated or had begun assembling cars in the United States. The amount of customs duties said to be lost by this assembly process became a significant political issue (this was when customs duties were the largest component of federal government revenues). There was political pressure to stop the practice. As a result, Panhard never assembled its cars here. However, the marque continued to be imported, with Smith & Mabley as their New York agents, and Quinby built bodies for some of them.

The December 1906 New York Automobile Show at Grand Central Palace included a number of Quinby open and closed body styles displayed on Panhard, Fiat, Renault, S&M Simplex and Mercedes chassis. Equally important was the critical assessment that Quinby was "...doing fully as well as the French makers..," a nice compliment at a time when European chassis and bodies were considered better quality than American.

The foreign automobile customs issue surely caught the eye of an aspiring Buffalo, N.Y., motor car manufacturer, the George N. Pierce Co., who was developing a line of Arrow cars to be a leading luxury marque. There was Francophile-like influence in the company which encouraged French suppliers and influence for both engines and body styles. For the 1905 model year, Pierce took the first series-custom step by offering a Quinby opera coach,

wheelbase chassis (with a 192-inch overall length). The Anderson family gave its cars names, also painting the family crest on the body sides together with the name and a saying. This Fiat was named "Il conquistadore" with the saying "Mil me pavet (nothing stops me)."

Anderson was a professional diplomat, suggesting the car was never raced despite its obvious potential

MEETING CHANGE AND CHALLENGE

The year 1909 was the 75th anniversary of the Quinby business; it also became the occasion to expand by representing chassis manufacturers. In early 1909, a showroom was leased in Philadelphia (at the intersection of Walnut and Twelfth streets), as the firm began representing Isotta Fraschini

Top inset: Quinby's Philadelphia branch advertised both automobiles and automobile bodies in 1911. Above: This group picture of the Brooks-Ostruk Co. annual outing at College Point, Long Island, on July 14, 1917, survives without an original caption. Emerson Brooks appears to be the fellow holding a large white hat, third in from the right. Paul Ostruk is also not clearly identified but appears to be to the right of Brooks. Right: This 1911 ad mixes a nifty slogan and logo.

with passengers entering from the rear of the vehicle. A second Quinby model, a landaulet, was also added to the Pierce catalog.

7 FIAT RUNABOUT

One of the most interesting examples of Quinby work survives at the Larz Anderson Auto Museum in Brookline, Mass. It is a large 1907 Fiat competition runabout. The big 11-liter 90hp four-cylinder engine is set into a long 139-inch

to do so. It was used both in Massachusetts and at Washington, D.C., the Anderson's main home. The Fiat still carries its original District of Colombia plates.

After Larz Anderson's death in 1927, his widow maintained his cars and the estate until her passing in 1948. Then, they became a museum. As a result, the Fiat remains a one-owner car - which helps explain its original paint, upholstery and heraldic trim. Much documentation survives, too. It is possible to trace its use through diaries of the family's tours.

and the Pennsylvania, an upper mid-price car built in nearby Bryn Mawr. This gave Quinby a captive audience for its bodies, something revealed in the firm's "For Sale" ads in the automobile section of the newspapers. At the time, Emerson Brooks, the treasurer of the Automobile Club of America and a vice president of Quinby, designed a new type of body, which inclined the front floor edge to help rest feet while driving. The body was built by Quinby on a Simplex chassis.

At the end of 1910, Quinby established another sales branch in Pennsylvania on Grand Boulevard in Pittsburgh, selling Simplex and Isotta-Fraschini cars. That coincided with problems with the Pennsylvania car; that marque soon went out of business. Quinby replaced the Pennsylvania's series-custom business with grander names, the Simplex and SGV. Still, behind the scenes, the Pennsylvania car business problems led to a lawsuit and other issues which detracted from the Quinby business. Despite this, Quinby continued to expand, adding a New York City showroom in Manhattan at 1849 Broadway.

Quinby was very good at creating splendor in an automobile body. For the January 1912 Importers' Salon in New York City, the company bodied two of the seven cars in the Benz exhibit (then a separate company from Mercedes), the largest in the show. The coronation of Great Britain's George V provided Quinby's theme. Described as "most striking" and "gorgeous" was a special 30hp "coronation limousine" painted "rich royal purple with gold striping." The roofline was specially constructed with a covered aluminum top. The interior was in gold fittings and gold leaf over mahogany woodwork, with mauve broadcloth upholstery. The crown of the King of England was set on the doors where one would expect to see a monogram. Equally intriguing was a 50hp "coronation torpedo" in the same color and trim combination, with specially-imported purple leather upholstery.

There was also great Quinby activity bodying Matheson "Silent Six" cars, big luxury vehicles with a 135-inch wheelbase chassis built in Wilkes-Barre, Pennsylvania. In the Spring of 1912, the Washington, D. C. salesroom of the Matheson Motor Company, at 1220 New York Avenue, had four cars on display, one of which was a Quinby berline limousine. Brewster & Co. also bodied some of the Mathesons there. It was an impressive showing - J. M. Boyd had been sent out from the Matheson factory to help with demonstrations. Unfortunately, 1912 was Matheson's last full year of production.

There were other aspects to Quinby's 1912 publicity, too. Emerson Brooks set forth a short primer about washing cars to readers of the New York Times. He pointed out that carriage and car bodies were both finished in varnish and should not be washed with soap. "Varnish is a soap in itself," he remarked. "Every time a vehicle is washed some of the surface is removed in the application of the alkali which is in dust and water. This effect is doubled when soap is added." There was no complete answer to this problem save revarnish, and that could be required as often as every two years. Brooks emphasized using a chamois cloth after washing was the most effective way to maintain a finish.

In May 1912, Isotta Fraschini took over sales of its cars in the United States. Losing such an exclusive distributorship must

Inset: This 1919 ad points out one of Brooks-Ostruk's specialities—rebodying old vehicles to look like new. Above: This Pierce-Arrow sedan/limousine demonstrates one of the the more conventional Brooks-Ostruk exterior designs. One of its features was a mattress concealed behind the driver's compartment. Below: The interior of a Minerva brougham built for Robert L. Corby, a director of the Fleischmann Yeast Company of New York. The shapes of the interior hardware are impressive.

have been a serious setback for Quinby. One cannot help but wonder if the company's prominence in the Benz display at the Salon led to some misgivings at Isotta; for those press accolades for the Coronation cars could have been about Isottas. Or, had Quinby anticipated Isotta's change and emphasized other marques?

Even so, Quinby remained one of four American coachbuilders—with Healey, Holbrook and Locke—exhibiting at the Importers' Automobile Show at New York's Astor Hotel in January 1913.

The January 1914 Importers' Automobile Salon reinforced Quinby's continued ability to dazzle. At the time, the largest passenger car engines were rated at 60 to 70hp or so, yet Isotta-Fraschini was offering a spectacular Model F rated at 120-130hp. So it was a very special treat to see the Isotta stand showing a Quinby enclosed-drive "social" limousine mounted on that chassis.

Above: Madame Alla Nazimova was said to be the highest-paid star in Hollywood when she took delivery of this extraordinary Rolls-Royce Silver Ghost with a body style called "sedan elite." The car was painted light blue with black fenders and no striping. Beneath the rear window reveals was the initial "N" in gold leaf.

first, the consequences of this issue were clouded by World War I.

The January 1915 Salon was unusual. World War I had begun, restricting the availability of cars. There were no automobiles exhibited from the Central Powers, but cars from the Allied Powers were there: Lancia and Peugeot were present. Quinby coachwork was limited to the Simplex exhibit, the only American marque on display. At the same time, the war in Europe encouraged a working relationship with the Wright Aeroplane Company; there was an announcement that the Simplex plant would be expanded with car production increased tenfold to 500 large cars and 800 smaller town cars. The Simplex engine was to be adapted for airplane use. Even so, the following year, Wright merged with Glenn L. Martin, and acquired the rights to the Hispano-Suiza airplane motor. That soon made Simplex automobile production redundant. At the same time, Leon Rubay's work became the center of automotive design - and he was able to accommodate a number of major automobile manufacturers at once. It is not clear why Quinby did not adjust to these changes, for there was plenty of war-related work in manufacturing. One explanation comes from a report that its owners wanted to retire.

With that, Quinby was never again among the coachbuilders with their own exhibits in the Salons - renamed the Automobile Salon to reflect the

dearth of foreign exhibitors. In March 1917, Quinby announced ending business. Its inventory - including items as diverse as Isotta-Fraschini parts, horse-drawn carriages and limousine speaking tubes - were sold at auction, for cash only, on Monday, July 2, 1917.

The prestige of the name led to reviving J. M. Quinby & Co. in June 1920, as only a commercial body company. The new business was located in East Orange, just outside Newark. It did not prosper. Early in 1929, the second Quinby business went into receivership.

BROOKS-OSTRUK

When Emerson Brooks, his wife Alice and Paul Ostruk founded Brooks-Ostruk in February 1917, they began with an artistic splash. The elaborate designs Brooks had drawn at Quinby shared the spotlight with shapes with hints of streamlining, a style we now associate with the work of Los Angeles, California, coachbuilders the Bentel Shops and Earl Coachworks (later Don Lee). Trendy and entertaining *Vanity Fair* noticed these designs as much as the coachbuilders' magazine, *Vehicle Monthly*.

Above: Robert Corby appears to have been a dedicated Brooks-Ostruk-bodied Minerva customer. He also bought this roadster called "Greyhound." It was painted Mediterranean Blue, striped with fine gold lines, and upholstered in crushed gray leather. Trim was finished in nickel.

Quinby's downfall appears to have been World War I. In late 1914, Simplex purchased another New Jersey luxury car maker, the Crane Motor Car Company, consolidating production at Simplex' New Brunswick factory. Crane's principal, Henry Crane, is said to have been partial to Brewster bodies. At

One of Brooks-Ostruk's trademarks was to remove the existing chassis radiator shell and replace it with a horseshoe-style design (similar to a Fiat), hiding the identity of the chassis manufacturer. There are a number of examples of this in Brooks-Ostruk's work; both Pierce-Arrow's radiator shell and distinctive fender-mounted headlights sometimes vanished this way.

The firm's initial showing at the January 1918 Automobile Salon in New York City, then still held in the ballroom of the Astor Hotel, exhibiting on a White chassis. What showed great promise included some disappointment: White shut down passenger car production shortly thereafter.

On April 24, 1920, Brooks-Ostruk decided to enlarge operations, something many other body builders were doing in response to increased postwar automobile demand. Capital was increased to $1,000,000, a level similar to the Rubay Company. Paul Ostruk went one step further and opened a Minerva agency in New York. Minerva had a modest popularity before World War I. About 215 cars had been sold in the United States, with most remaining in service after the War.

At the Automobile Salons, Brooks-Ostruk displayed some of the most imaginative designs. Delage was being introduced to the American market; the firm designed a splendid one-of-a-kind "sporting trap" body, painted "light mocha," which was shown at the November 1920 Salon in New York City. Its simple elegant lines, set off with a thick beltline, were made unusual by single wide side doors set between the front and rear seats.

There were reports of Brooks-Ostruk building the first American bodies for Rolls-Royce of America (a licensee of the British firm). Rolls adapted to the United States market gradually; it did not present American-style bodies on a series-custom basis until later in the 1920s. However, Brooks-Ostruk records survive confirming two Brooks-Ostruk bodies set on postwar Derby Silver Ghost chassis: (1) a limousine delivered in February 1920 and (2) a Salamanca cabriolet delivered to C. B. Stevens at 30 E. 58th Street,

Above: This stunning body, another version of the "sedan elite," was built on a 1921 Minerva chassis for actress Billie Burke (Mrs. Florenz Ziegfeld). It was conspicuously trimmed with all-white tires, wire wheels, a polished metal hood, and a glossy light-colored leather roof. The interior was upholstered in morocco goatskin with inlays by Driguet of Paris. **Below:** Brooks-Ostruk displayed this Minerva town car during the November 1921 New York Automobile Salon, where it was characterized as the show's "artistic gem." The body was light gray with a darker shade of gray in the soft leather top. The interior matched the body with a broadcloth interior and gray fittings. It was purchased by Ziegfeld Follies' star Marilynn Miller.

New York City in October 1920. The best known of these cars matched the fame of their owners - such as the one ordered by actress Madame Alla Nazimova.

Unfortunately, the severe 1921 recession played havoc with demand for these great cars. Many expensive chassis makers such as Pierce-Arrow and Marmon were in financial trouble; Lincoln and Lafayette were unable to remain in business as independent companies.

The most expensive car in the world in 1921 - and certainly the most publicized - was bodied by Brooks-Ostruk. It was an armored limousine on a Packard Twin Six chassis, built for $35,000 for the Tsan Tso-Lin, the Governor General of Manchuria. The specifications were demanding - armored to be bulletproof yet capable of looking very ceremonial. "The car can be transformed in a twinkling," observed Vehicle Monthly. Windows were shielded by metal shutters on rollers (much like today's hurricane shutters); gun ports were set into the sides of the passenger compartment. A machine gun set into

the windshield could be removed and set underneath the dash. It was said 18 months was needed to plan and build the car.

THE 1921 AUTOMOBILE SALON

The combination of Minerva dealership and coachbuilding business led Brooks-Ostruk to dominate the November 1921 Salon. The four Minervas displayed in the Commodore's East Ballroom—a brougham, a cabriolet, a limousine and a sedan—had Brooks-Ostruk bodies. They emphasized that the firm was seeking the business of prominent persons at home, too. Ziegfeld Follies' star Marilynn Miller bought the cabriolet. Miller soon became known for her town cars; her enthusiastic fans sometimes ordered exact copies of her cars to be made for themselves. Perhaps Miller had an arrangement with Brooks-Ostruk concerning this.

Also interesting was the adjacent Minerva in

the exhibit, a two-window sedan elite, built for the wife of Miller's boss, Florenz Ziegfeld. At this time, Ziegfeld's off-stage relationship with Miller led to widely publicized problems (excerpts from his telegrams to his wife about it were printed in the New York newspapers) with his famous wife, Billie Burke. Burke won when Miller left the Follies to marry Mary Pickford's brother. The details of this situation, which could have been elaborately-planned publicity, have yet to be revealed. We suspect Brooks-Ostruk knew what they were.

A highly judgmental view of Brooks-Ostruk's work at that Salon came from coachbuilder and competitor Thomas Hibbard, then a partner with Raymond Dietrich in LeBaron, Inc., writing in *Art & Decoration* magazine. Hibbard was intrigued by the Boyriven broadcloth upholstery and marquetry in the rear doors of a Minerva town car. His comments on the pillow-like cushions in the passenger compartment (such as in the Corby Minerva on page xxx) seemed too critical, pointing out that they were "...most comfortable for short runs," but not for a journey of several hours. He suggested cushions should be made using a practice seen in horse-drawn carriages - "a slight squabbing of down over curled hair." Hibbard had worked for master coachbuilder Leon Rubay in the Teens; his comments had proven technical expertise.

Brooks-Ostruk bodies were seen on the West Coast of the United States, too. Alla Nazimova, the "illustrious tragedienne" of motion pictures, was the highest-paid actress in Hollywood in 1920. She was also a style-arbiter for the movie colony. Her order for a two-window "sedan elite" on a Rolls-Royce Silver Ghost chassis, painted "an exquisite shade of light blue" with black fenders and top, made an impressive statement. There was no body stripe; Mme. Nazimova's initial "N" was set in gold leaf on the rear door, beneath the window reveal. Inside was upholstered in tan broadcloth and ribbed silk upholstery with fittings described as "genuine old ivory."

Equally interesting commissions were made for second bodies. The Vanderbilt family in Hyde Park,

Above: The Manchurian warlord Tsan So Lin ordered this Packard Twin Six limousine painted in shades of brown and tan with moldings edged in a line of gold and black. It was the most expensive automobile in the world; one estimate of its cost was $30,000. The interior was breathtaking: seats were upholstered in figured gold and purple mohair; the mahogany paneling had silver and cloisonné fittings. The doors were inlaid with flowered parquetry created from 20 varieties of wood. Opposite: 1922 Minerva AM seven-passenger sedan bodied by Paul Ostruk.

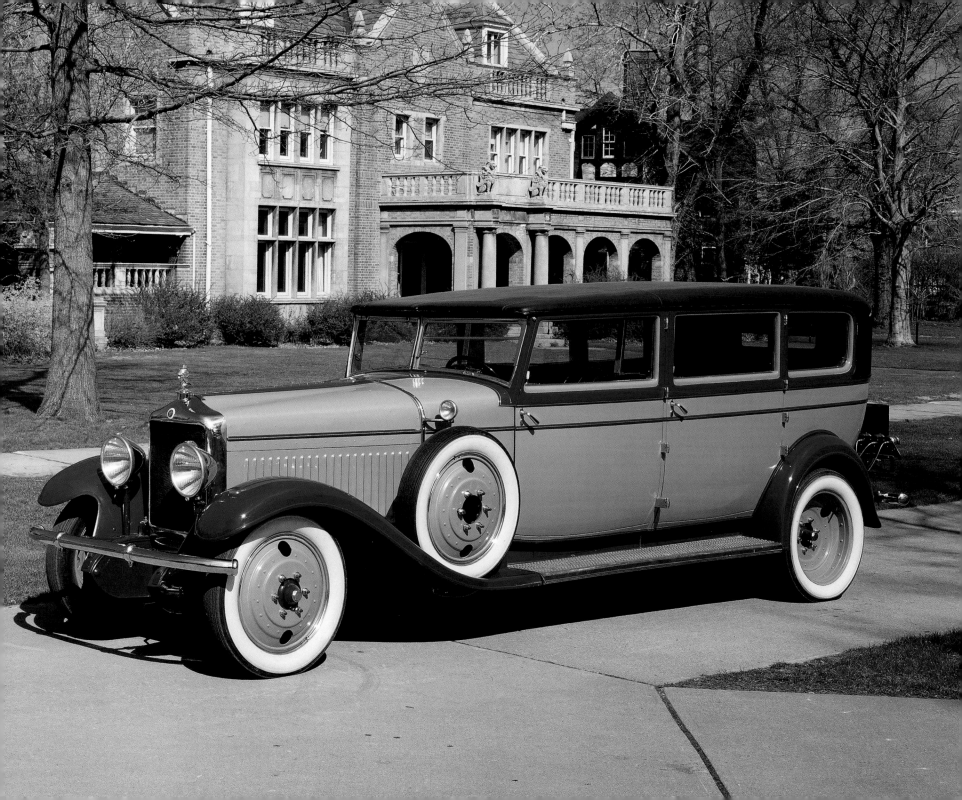

Above and far right: One of the last of Paul Ostruk's bodies, on a 1932 Minerva AL town car.

New York, owned an elegant 1918 Crane-Simplex fitted with a Brewster touring car body. One day, as the car was being driven from their Manhattan town house to Hyde Park, they met a neighbor's car and decided to race. The wind and drafts from the high speeds that day were said to irritate Mrs. Vanderbilt. She contacted Brooks-Ostruk and ordered a closed body put on the chassis, to preclude being in that situation again.

What is interesting is that the sedan elite body chosen was a catalog style, although a series-cus-

tom design, many trim variations were made. The sedan name understated its most dramatic feature: the blind rear quarter not only shielded those in the rear compartment from onlookers; it provided them with the wonderful camera obscura-style view of the road, one that is usually associated with the town car body style.

The November 1922 New York Automobile Salon was Brooks-Ostruk's last. The firm displayed six designs, some more conventional than others. Emerson Brooks must have reminisced about the

show's center of attention—a limousine painted celestial blue, with black moldings and fenders, on an Isotta-Fraschini chassis—as Isotta had been one of Quinby's most important clients. Brooks-Ostruk's Locomobile coupe with a sloping windshield and a Peerless cabriolet were also significant.

This was when Locomobile had recently purchased by Durant Motors. The coupe acted as a prototype for the firm's designs. The Peerless cabriolet was developed from the standard Brooks-Ostruk body shell with colorful trimming, not as under-

Above: In front of the 225-227 West 66th Street Brooks-Ostruk premises in Manhattan, showing a number of cars displayed in the November 1922 Automobile Salon.

stated as Marilynn Miller's cabriolet. It was one of a series of specially designed cars created by different coachbuilders signaling Peerless' attempt to again be one of the leading luxury marques in the United States. However, continued management changes at Peerless ended this luxury refocus; the marque spent the remainder of the 1920s without its prewar opulence.

The three bodies on Minerva chassis foretold a change in the company's direction. At the November 1923 Salon, Paul Ostruk exhibited them under his own name. He retained the West 66th Street premises as a service station, repeating what the Quinby busi-

ness had done two decades earlier, becoming agent for a chassis manufacturer—the Minerva. Radio pioneer Thomas Garvan was one of Ostruk's investors; a Park Avenue showroom was added to the business. Unlike Quinby, Ostruk soon decided against bodying the cars himself, and had coachbuilders such as Rollston and Le Baron create custom and series-custom bodies for him. That led the Brooks-Ostruk business to last only several years, a sharp comparison to the Quinby existence, which measured its business activity in decades.

The death of Emerson Brooks' wife Alice in April 1924 changed his professional direction. He

decided to wind up his automotive business affairs and left his home in Montclair, N.J., moving south to Trenton. He went on to a second career founding the Boy Rangers of America, an organization for pre-Scout-age boys. It grew to 200,000 members at the time of his death in 1948.

In the late 1920s, Paul Ostruk expanded his focus on selling Minervas, buying Hibbard & Darrin's French distributorship in Paris. In 1932, as the Depression destroyed demand worldwide for Minervas, his New York business was forced into bankruptcy. **AQ**

WALT HANSGEN
His Life and the History of Post-War American Road Racing

By Michael Argetsinger

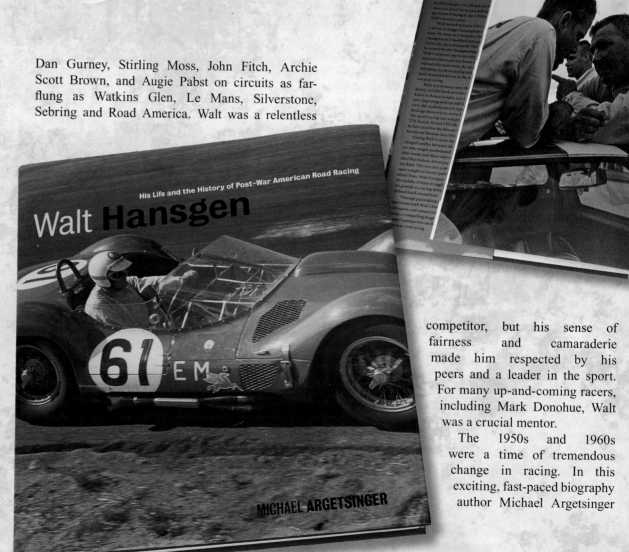

W alt Hansgen was a star in both sports cars and single-seaters, and his meteoric career carried him from the early days of amateur road racing to the very highest level of professional competition in America and Europe.

As the lead driver on Briggs Cunningham's dominant team, and later John Mecom's team, Walt evaluated and developed race cars working closely with Jaguar, Lister, Maserati and Ford. At different points in his career he paired with Dan Gurney, Stirling Moss, John Fitch, Archie Scott Brown, and Augie Pabst on circuits as far-flung as Watkins Glen, Le Mans, Silverstone, Sebring and Road America. Walt was a relentless competitor, but his sense of fairness and camaraderie made him respected by his peers and a leader in the sport. For many up-and-coming racers, including Mark Donohue, Walt was a crucial mentor.

The 1950s and 1960s were a time of tremendous change in racing. In this exciting, fast-paced biography author Michael Argetsinger

LEFT: John Mecom (left) and Walt stand in front of the Scarab at Mecom team headquarters in Houston. Walt became the lead driver for the Mecom Racing Team in 1964. (Mel Anderson: John Mecom Collection)

BOTTOM LEFT: After winning at Galveston in 1964 for Mecom Racing, Walt set out on the victory lap in the Lotus 19B-Olds. (Hansgen Family Collection)

BOTTOM RIGHT: Walt is on his way to a third place finish in the McKinney Ford Galaxie in the NASCAR Grand National race at Watkins Glen in 1964. Walt made a strong impression as the regulars in his three races at NASCAR's top level. (Ade Ketchum Collection)

RIGHT: The MG Liquid Suspension Special in the pits during a practice day at Indy 1965. Walt again showed great speed in his second race at the brickyard. (Hansgen Family Collection)

BELOW: Walt, wearing his "honorary Texan" hat, poses with the Mecom Racing Team Ferrari 250 LM at Bridgehampton for the 1964 FIA 500. Walt won the race in the Scarab and Augie Pabst drove the Ferrari. (Hansgen Family Collection)

LEFT: At speed in the Lotus 33 Formula 1 car during the 1964 United States Grand Prix at Watkins Glen. Walt scored World Championship points for Team Lotus with a fine fifth-place finish. (Hansgen Family Collection)

The book is handsomely illustrated with previously unpublished photos from the Hangsen family's collection and the collections of others who were close to Walt. These images from 1964-65 depict the depth and diversity of Walt's career racing sports cars, Indy cars, Formula 1 and NASCAR. His racing relationship with John Mecom (upper left) was especially fruitful.

shows how Walt's life encompassed the conflict between amateur and professional racing, the extraordinary advances in technology, and the joyful ambition of his era. The result is a vivid account of the remarkable history of post-war American road racing.

ALSO AVAILABLE: THE PUBLISHER'S EDITION of Walt Hansgen: His Life and the History of Post-War American Road Racing. All proceeds will benefit the International Motor Racing Research

Center at Watkins Glen. The signatories are a veritable "Who's Who" in American racing, including Cameron Argetsinger, John Bishop, John Fitch, Dan Gurney, Bea Hansgen, John Mecom, Augie Pabst, and the author. This edition is offered in a numbered series limited to just 150. $225. Numbers 1-50 are bound in superior garment-quality leather. $375.

Walt Hansgen: His Life and the History of Post-War American Road Racing

Hardcover, 8 3/8 x 9 in., 400 pages
Photos: 15 color, 140 black-and-white
ISBN 1-893618-54-4
$49.95

Available from Automobile Quarterly:
Tel.: (812) 948-2886
Fax: (812) 948-2816

NOTES AND N&C COMMENTARY

CONTACTING AQ
Automobile Quarterly, ISSN 0005-1438, ISBN 1-59613-050-4 (978-1-59613-050-0), is published quarterly by Automobile Heritage Publishing and Communications, LLC. Editorial and publication offices: 800 East 8th Street, New Albany, Indiana, USA 47150. Telephone (812) 948-AUTO (2886); fax (812) 948-2816; e-mail info@autoquarterly.com; Web site www.autoquarterly.com.

SUBSCRIPTION SERVICE
For subscriptions, back issues, indexes, reader service, changes of address, and order entry, call (866) 838-2886. If calling from Indiana or outside the U.S., call (812) 948-2886. Back issue prices start at $25.95, plus shipping. For domestic subscription orders: 1 year (4 issues), $79.95; 2 years (8 issues), $149.95; 3 years (12 issues), $199.95. for Canadian orders: 1 year, $99.95; 2 years, $189.95; 3 years, $259.95. For all other international orders: 1 year, $109.95; 2 years, $209.95; 3 years, $289.95. Mastercard, Visa, or American Express are accepted. Order online at www.autoquarterly.com. To order by mail, please send check or money order to *AQ/Automobile Quarterly*, 1950 Classic Car Circle, P.O. Box 1950, New Albany, IN 47151. The fax number for orders is (812) 948-2816.

POSTMASTER
Please send all changes of address to: *Automobile Quarterly*, P.O. Box 1950, New Albany, IN 47151. Periodical postage paid at New Albany, Indiana, and at additional mailing offices.

LEGAL NOTICE
Entire contents copyright 2005 by Automobile Heritage Publishing and Communications, LLC. Library of Congress Catalog Number 62-4005. *AQ, Automobile Quarterly*, Quatrafoil, and are registered trademarks of Automobile Heritage Publishing and Communications, LLC. All rights reserved. Reproduction in whole or in part without permission is prohibited.

OPPORTUNITY
Details of fund raising programs for car clubs and automobile museums are available by calling: (812) 948-AUTO (2886).

Cover & Contents
Art by Dennis Brown.

Frontispiece
Color photography by Charles S. White, from the AQ Photo and Research Archives, p. 1.

The Blue Goose
Special thanks to: The Carnlough Trust; the Don F. Pratt Museum; Chris Charlton at Classic Car Services; Herbert F. von Fragstein; James P. Champion; and Joe Crilley.

Black-and-white photography: pp. 5, 6 (left), p. 6 (right), 10, 11 (right) courtesy of the U.S. National Archives; p. 7 courtesy of James Champion; p. 9 courtesy of the U.S. Army, Dan F. Pratt Museum, Fort Campbell, Ky.; p. 11 (left) from the *Indianapolis Star*.

Color photography: pp. 4, 7, 10, 12 (right), 13, 14, 15 by Maine Photo Express, courtesy of Classic Car Services and The Carnlough Trust; p. 8 courtesy of Joe Crilley; p. 12 (left) courtesy of the U.S. Army, Dan F. Pratt Museum, Fort Campbell, Ky.

Bibliography
Irving, David. *Goering, A Biography*. William Morrow and Co., 1989, New York;

Melin, Jan. *Mercedes-Benz, the Supercharged 8-cylinder Cars of the 1930s, Volume 1*. Norlook International, Gothenburg, Sweden, 1985;

Jan Melin and Sven Hernstrom. *Mercedes-Benz, the Supercharged 8-cylinder Cars of the 1930s, Volume 2*. Gamla Bisalongen AB, Sparreholm, Sweden, 2003;

Shirer, William L. *The Rise and Fall of the Third Reich: A History of Nazi Germany*. Exter Books, U.S.A., 1987;

Struhlemmer, Rupert. *85 Jahre Berliner Automobil, Ausftellungen 1897-1982*. Dalton Watson Ltd., London, 1982;

Taylor, Blaine. *Mercedes-Benz Parade and Staff Cars of the Third Reich*. Combined Publishing, Pennsylvania, U.S., 1999.

Art Gallery with Dennis Brown
The author would like to thank this issue's artist, Dennis Brown, for his time spent on the phone and preparing his art for publication in AQ.

Color photography courtesy of Dennis Brown.

Giugiaro's Bugattis
The author thanks Giorgetto Giugiaro, Franco Bay, Lorenza Cappello, Georges Keller, Julius Kruta, Dr. Ferdinand Piëch, and Adriana Crosetto, who conducted translations during the Giugiaro interview.

Color photography from the Gavin Farmer Collection and courtesy of Volkswagen.

Bibliography
Alfieri, Bruno, pub. *Car Men—Giorgetto Giugiaro & Fabrizio: Italdesign*. Automobilia, 1995;

Ciferri, Luca. *Italdesign: Thirty Years on the Road*. Formagrafica Edizioni, 1998;

Motor Buch Verlag. *Design by Giugiaro*. Edition Autofocus, 2003;

Research also sourced *EVO* magazine.

Art Ross
For sharing their memories, both personal and professional, the author thanks Art's son, Carter, and past designer Bernie Smith. Special thanks also to the Benson Ford Research Center for its magnificent contribution to automotive history in the preservation and digitization of its Automotive Design Oral History, from which interesting tidbits of designers' interaction with Art Ross confirmed personal recollection.

Black-and-white photography courtesy of Carter Ross.

Color photography: pp. 40, 41, 42, 43, 52, 53 courtesy of Carter Ross; pp. 46-47, 50-51, 54-55 from the AQ Photo and Research Archives.

Bibliography
Armi, C. Edson. *The Art of American Car Design: The Profession and Personalities*. The Pennsylvania State University Press, University Park and London, 1988;

Bayley, Stephen. *Harley Earl*. Taplinger Publishing Company, New York, 1990;

Harley Earl as told to Arthur W. Baum. "I Dream Automobiles." *The Saturday Evening Post*, Aug. 7, 1954;

Richard Langworth and Jan Norbye. *The Complete History of General Motors, 1908-1986*. Consumer Guide, 1986;

Jan Norbye and Jim Dunne. *Oldsmobile: The Postwar Years*. Motorbooks International, Osceola, Wisconsin, 1981;

United States Patent Office, Design Nos. 157623, 159929, 160128, 154638, 159930, 160127, 154639, 160661.

Last of the Big Packards
The author would like to thank Mark Patrick, Laura Kotsis and Barbara Thompson of the National Automotive History Collection of the Detroit Public Library, Kim Miller of the AACA Library and Research Center, Zoe Mayho of LAT Photographic, John McIlroy of Autosport, Hugo Mabbott of The Autocar, Arthur Stone's Ft. Lauderdale Antique Car Museum, the staff of the Benson Ford Library and Research Center of The Henry Ford, Ann Reich of Automotive News and Emily Foley for R. L. Polk & Co. for their help. John MacArthur and Jon Ottman of the Packard Motor Car Foundation (www.packardmotorfdn.org) provided a great deal of information. Stuart Blond, George Hamlin, Dan Hall and Larry Dopps also shared information and experiences with the last big Packards. Former Packard employees Carl Altz and Dwight Heinmuller shared photographs of the Packard Proving Grounds testing of the cars. The staff of the Library of Congress also helped obtain historic background material from its periodicals collections.

Black-and-white photography: pp. 58, 59, 62, 63 from the AQ Photo and Research Archives; pp. 66 (left), 67 (right) courtesy of Carl Altz and the Packard Motor Car Foundation; pp. 66 (right), 67 (left) courtesy of Dwight Heinmuller and the Packard Motor Car Foundation.

Color photography: pp. 56, 58, 59, 60, 61, 64 from the AQ Photo and Research Archives; pp. 62, 65 courtesy of the AACA Library and Research Center.

Packard Museums
The author wishes to thank Terry Martin and Robert Signom for sharing their time and abundant information on Packard, and the

(cont. on page 124)

A Snap-on Truck
Every Living Roc

Or home office, or den, or wherever y
computer is.

We've made it easy for enthusiasts ev
to find the Snap-on tools they would
have for their cars, boats, motorcycle
other toys. Log on to www.snapon.c
choose from more than 14,000 profes
quality tools, tool boxes, and test ins
the same tools that professionals ev
stake their reputations on every day
deliver them right to your door. Yo
will never be the same.

Snap-on.c

Concours d'elegan[ce]
at KEENEL[AND]

Showplace of Thoroughbred Horse[...]

Plan now to be at one of [...]
most unique settings for a [...]
Concours...the beautiful, [...]
historic grounds of
KEENELAND RACE C[...]
the internationally ren[...]
home of the Bluegras[...]
The Concours d'elegan[...]
KEENELAND Aug. 25-2[...]
in Lexington, Kentucky w[...]
one you will always reme[...]

For more information:
Call 859-422-3329
www.lexingtonconcours[...]

Cox Auctions presents

THE BRANSON COLLECTOR CAR AUCTION

OCTOBER 20, 21 AND 22, 2006

Missouri's Premier Collector Car Auction

For Bidding or Consignment Information:
WWW.BRANSONAUCTION.COM OR 800-335-3063

COX AUCTIONS

BRANSON MISSOURI

museums both gentlemen serve. Thanks also to Arthur Stone at the Fort Lauderdale Antique Car Museum. The author is presently a senior editor with the trade publication *American Machinist*, and is former editor-in-chief of the trade publication *Designfax*.

Color photography: pp.68-78 by Patrick Ertel and Suzanne Stevens; p.79 courtesy of the Fort Lauderdale Antique Car Museum.

Contact Information

The National Packard Museum
1899 Mahoning Avenue NW
P.O. Box 1416
Warren, Ohio 44482
Tel.: (330) 394-1899
Fax: (330) 394-7796

The Citizens Motorcar Company
420 South Ludlow Street
Dayton, Ohio 45402
Tel.: (937) 226-1710
Fax: (937) 224-1918

Fort Lauderdale Antique Car Museum
1527 Packard Avenue (SW 1st Avenue)
Ft. Lauderdale, Florida 33315
Tel.: (954) 779-7300
Fax: (954) 779-2501

Motoring Through the 1940s

Heading into this third part of our series on Motoring Through Tough Times, it seemed that this section on World War Two would be the easiest to figure. Politics couldn't be much at issue, and the old stories of the automobile industry's Homefront heroism were well documented. Then I found the story of the woman who was thankful at the end of rationing because she wouldn't have to steal gasoline anymore. No, no, no! This wouldn't be so easy. Indeed, as with any time, the 1940s were complicated. Multiply it by a nation entirely mobilized for war and an uneasy, unruly, and impatient recovery back to peace, and the telling of it ought never to end.

I wish to thank the good folks who shared their wartime stories, starting with my parents who, although young at the time, remember a thing or two. Mom's clearest memory is of when they lit up the Capitol after V-E Day. Dad's is of watching his father try to dissemble his Military Police machine gun in the living room in Carmel, California. A spring shot off and broke a window! Thankfully, Captain, and, later, Colonel, Charles D. Bromley proved far more useful to his country by applying his great legal mind to the Reverse Lend-Lease program with Australia and serving as the American representative to the Pacific Defense Council. On General MacArthur's staff after the war, he helped write the Japanese Constitution.

I also wish to thank my uncle Douglas Ladd for his magnificent stories of, as a young man just mustered out of the Navy after serving on a landing ship in the Pacific theater, hunting down leftover Cadillac limousines and other great Classic Era cars that nobody else wanted (they weren't "classic cars" yet...). He ran the damned things as a lark, and what fun he had! I ought to have written the entire article on him. Like all of us, his was but a fine angle on the rest. God bless ya, Uncle Dud!

Black-and-white photography: pp. 80, 84 (bottom) courtesy of Ford Motor Company and Wieck Media Services, Inc.; pp. 81 courtesy of the National Archives; pp. 82, 83, 84 (top), 85, 86, 87, 88, 89 courtesy of the Library of Congress.
Color photography: pp. 86, 87 courtesy of the Library of Congress; p. 89 courtesy of Ford Motor Company and Wieck Media Services, Inc.

Bibliography

Automotive and Aviation Industries, Chilton Class Journal Company, Philadelphia, PA, 1941-1950;
Chicago Tribune, Chicago Tribune Company, 1941-1947;
Hamburg, D., "The Recession of 1948-49 in the United States," *The Economic Journal,* March, 1952, pp. 1-14;
New York Times, H.J. Raymond & Co., 1941-1953;
Rae, John B., *The American Automobile: A Brief History,* University of Chicago Press, Chicago, 1965;
Vatter, Harold G., "The Closure of Entry in the American Automobile Industry," Oxford Economic Papers, Oct. 1952, pp. 213-234.

Gold's Garage

Special thanks to Stanley Gold for opeing his garage doors for the world to see. It's quite a place!
Color photography by the author.

Concours d'Elegance Villa d'Este

The author wishes to extend his gratitude especially to Urs Paul Ramseier, president of the Swiss Car Register and responsible for the selection of participating cars in the Villa d'Este event in the past five years. He generously provided official documents and information. Personal talks with participants and visitors as well as with the photographer, Michel Zumbrunn, also were helpful and appreciated.

Black-and-white photography courtesy of Michel Zumbrunn.
Color photography by Michel Zumbrunn.

Bibliography

Anselmi, Angelo Tito, ed. *Villa d'Este: The Italian Concours.* 2004;
Other primary sources include official Concorso d'Eleganza Villa d'Este lists of participants and cars; program and regulations; lists of award winners; press releases by BMW Group and the illustrated program booklets, 2000-2005. Also sourced were reports and articles in various motoring and automobile magazines published in Italy, France, U.K., Germany and Switzerland.

Quinby/Brooks-Ostruk

A number of people have helped assemble the materials that are here. The author would like to thank Mark Patrick, Barbara Thompson and Laura Kotsis of the National Automotive History Collection of the Detroit Public Library; Kim Miller of the AACA Library and Research Center; Joe Freeman and John Sweeney of the Larz Anderson Museum; and Anne Jordan and Frank Futral of the Vanderbilt Mansion (National Park Service) in Hyde Park, New York. Fred Roe shared his knowledge of the Simplex. Keith Marvin and Warren Kraft also offered their knowledge of this era. John W. deCampi, Andre Blaize and Steve Hubbard helped with Rolls-Royce information. As always, the staff of the Library of Congress helped in obtaining historic background material from its collections.

Black-and-white photography: pp. 108 (left), 109 (top) from the Detroit Public Library, National Automotive History Collection; pp. 108 (right), 110 (group photo), 111 (bottom), 112, 113, 114, 117 courtesy of the AACA Library and Research Center; p. 109 (bottom) courtesy of the Larz Anderson Auto Museum; p. 110 (insets), 111 (inset) courtesy of the Library of Congress.
Color photography: pp. 106, 115, 116, 117 from the AQ Photo and Research Archives.

Bibliography

"A Luxurious Armored Limousine." *Vehicle Monthly,* July 1921;
"American Coachwork Dominates DeLuxe Models In New York Salon." *Motor World,* December 13, 1922;
"Auto Body Concern Is in Receivership." *Newark Evening News,* March 7, 1929;
"Big Automobile Plant In Newark, *New York Herald,* September 5, 1899;
"Emerson Brooks, 87, Auto Body Pioneer." *New York Herald Tribune,* July 24, 1948;
"Exclusive Bodywork On American and Foreign Cars." *Motor,* January 1922;
Hibbard, Thomas, L. "An Exhibition of Motor Cars and Bodies of the New Mode." *Art & Decoration,* January 1922;
"In The Automobile World." *Washington Post,* April 8, 1912;
Oxberry, Sydney. "The Undated Car is Here." *Motor,* July 1920;
Ozias, Blake. "Forecast of the November Automobile Salon." *Arts & Decoration,* November 1920;
"Panhard Automobiles In America." *Wall Street Journal,* January 14, 1903;
Pfau, Hugo. *The Custom Body Era.* A.S. Barnes and Co., 1970;
Sutton, George, W., Jr. "The Theatrical Taste In Motor Cars." *Motor Life,* September 1922;
"The Automobile Salon." *Motor Travel,* January 1920;
"The Importers' Salon." *The Club Journal,* December 24, 1910;
"The Importers' Salon." *The Club Journal,* February 1915;
"The 1920 New York Automobile Salon," *Vehicle Monthly,* January 1921;
"Washing Autos An Art." *New York Times,* December 2, 1912.

Coda

Color photography by Suzanne Stevens.

Back Cover

Debossment of the AQ logo from the AQ Photo and Research Archives.

THE CARS THAT HENRY FORD BUILT

*A Commemorative Tribute
To America's Most
Remembered Automobiles*

by BEVERLY RAE KIMES

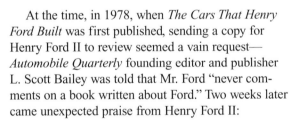

At the time, in 1978, when *The Cars That Henry Ford Built* was first published, sending a copy for Henry Ford II to review seemed a vain request—*Automobile Quarterly* founding editor and publisher L. Scott Bailey was told that Mr. Ford "never comments on a book written about Ford." Two weeks later came unexpected praise from Henry Ford II:

> *"My grandfather would
> have liked this book."*

Ford then specially ordered 20 copies bound in white leather—needed in two weeks. The rushorder was necessitated by an upcoming trip to Japan. As is culturally customary to offer a gift that honors one's ancestors, Henry Ford II specifically chose *The Cars That Henry Ford Built* to give to his Japanese hosts.

Such high-level praise is derived from the book's fresh approach to the subject of Henry Ford, both in its study of the man and his cars, as well as the exceptional pictorial presentation. Presented for the first time in full color, there is every model Henry Ford produced from the Quadricycle he put together as a young man in 1896 to the famous V8 Ford on the production lines four and a half decades later during his failing years.

Probably no other individual in automotive history more accurately mirrored in the essence of his cars his view of himself, and of America as he saw it. Join award-winning historian and author Beverly Rae Kimes as she presents lively historical text that captures Henry Ford growing and aging as his cars grew and aged, each lock-stepped together through history. More than 100 full-color photographs further bring the man and his creations to life.

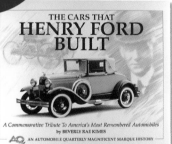

When Timing is Everything

The fabled collection of James Ward Packard's pocket watches is well known to Packard historians and watch collectors alike. Perhaps the finest collection of pocket watches ever assembled was gifted to the Smithsonian Institution in 1928 upon Ward Packard's death.

But for years Packard aficionados have whispered about the equally legendary "one that got away": Ward Packard's personal timepiece, the one that did not go to the Smithsonian as part of the collection, the one still out there, somewhere.

On the occasion of his 53rd birthday on Nov. 5, 1916, Ward Packard was presented with a very special gift, indeed, presumably by his wife. It is engraved on the inside cover: "James Ward Packard, Warren, Ohio, Nov. 5th 1916." Purchased from the Myers & Trefry Jewelers in hometown Warren, the 17-jewel Witnauer Minute Repeater was perhaps the finest pocket watch

of its day. With an 18-karat gold and sterling case, and Ward's monogram emblazed on the back cover in midnight blue cloisonné, the exquisite timepiece was, and is, a sight to behold.

How did the "one that got away" get away? As Ward's personal timepiece, why was it not shipped to Washington for inclusion in the Smithsonian collection? And how did it resurface, as Packard collectors had hoped for decades that it might?

The first two answers are simple. Instead of being shipped off to Washington, the special Witnauer was shipped off to New York—specifically to the Packard summer home at Lake Chautauqua.

Although showing so little wear as to virtually guarantee that Ward did not carry it on a daily basis, the watch was clearly important to him, not as a part of his collection, but rather as a personal keepsake. After his death it remained at the Chautauqua house,

until the family only recently sold the property.

The end of the story is as fascinating as the beginning. When the Packard family sold the Chautauqua property, either they or the new owners had a tag sale to dispose of the personal property in the house, and the Witnauer was included. A local antique collector purchased the watch for a few hundred dollars, and later listed it for sale on eBay with a minimum bid of $1,500 and no reserve. He also incorrectly listed it as "pocket watch of John Packard, Auto Magnate." It attracted no interest whatsoever from Packard collectors, and generated only two bids: $1,500 from a "non-Packard" watch guy, and $1,510 from America's Packard Museum Founder and Curator Bob Signom. It is still in the original presentation box from the jeweler.

Sometimes you are in the right place at the right time. **AQ**